'SPEAK WELSH'

An introduction to the Welsh language combining a simple grammar, phrase book and dictionary

JOHN JONES

"Speak Welsh" First published 1977 by John Jones Cardiff Ltd
Republished by John Jones Publishing Ltd, 1983
New square-spine edition, March 1998
New edition with new material, April 2002

This edition with new material, April 2005
Reprinted May 2011
Reprinted May 2014
Reprinted February 2016
Reprinted March 2018

ISBN 1 871083 00 1

Illustrations by Eric Jones, Carmarthen

Printed by Cambrian Printers, Llanbadarn Road, Aberystwyth, SY23 3TN

Published by John Jones Publishing Ltd@live.com

A Historical Introduction to Welsh

People in Wales today speak a language which is very different from English and is much older. This language "*Cymraeg*" is part of a Celtic family of language: its close relations are Cornish and Breton, the former previously spoken in Cornwall, the latter still spoken in Brittany. Welsh is more distantly related to the Gaelic languages still spoken in parts of Ireland and Scotland, and previously on the Isle of Man. Today the Welsh-speaking people of Wales call themselves *Cymry*, a word which links them to the Irish, Scots and Cornish, meaning 'people of this country', with reference to a time before various immigrant tongues combined to make the English Language.

The Welsh language remained with the Celtic people who fled westwards, away from the Anglo-Saxons. They remained in the area now called Wales, protected by rough land and mountains. The survival of this language in Wales is a linguistic phenomenon, and today we see one of the oldest languages on earth existing side-by-side with English, one of the newest.

The ealiest history of Britain is a tale of successive invasions. The Roman colonisation of Britain started in 43 AD, and evidence of Roman civilisation is found in the extensive road networks, sites of archaeological interests, coins, forts and constructions, the most famous being Hadrian's Wall. It is interesting to speculate on what sort of mix of Celtic the original tribes spoke, but the two tribes, the Brythoniaid (Britons) and the Goidels (Irish) separated and their related tongues developed separately. The Celtic tongue survived the Romans, who finally withdrew their legions in AD 410, but some Latin terms remained. The Welsh word *braich* (arm) derives from the Latin *bracchia*, whereas coes (leg) derives from the Celtic word *cosca*. Similarly one can see the influence of Latin through the similarity of certain French and Welsh words, e.g. *ffenestr* (window) and French *fenetre*; porth (dorway) and *porte*; un, dau, tri (one, two, three) and *un, deux, trois*.

The old Brythoneg developed into three separate languages, Welsh, Cornish and Breton. Cornish fell out of common use in the eighteenth century.

The Anglo-Saxon Chronicle says that the first invaders after the Romans - the Angles, Saxons and Jutes - sailed across the sea from Denmark and the coastal stretch of Germany, in AD 449. The native Britons were driven north and west, beaten by fierce and warlike people. This was the beginning of English as a language, but the 'Old English' period was followed by Middle English'. Only in the period of Geoffrey Chaucer in the fourteenth century do we see the beginning of English as we know it now.

The Angles and Saxons invaded what is now the North of England. Many fierce battles were fought between the *Cymry* and the new invaders. There was one famous battle at Manau Gododdin, the present-day Sterling. The earliest poetry in Welsh dates from this period; the text has been preserved on carefully-kept mediaeval manuscripts.

The *Cymry* who lived in what is now England were partly absorbed into the society and culture of the Angles and Saxons. Marriages amongst these people took place and finally the Cymry lost their language and culture in the central areas. However, other groups of Cymry withdrew to the west protected by harsh terrain, so a language which was spoken by people in what is now England and possibly parts of Scotland, is now only spoken in its modern form by a group of people in Wales.

The process of forcing the British into the 'Celtic fringe' did not happen quickly. One major successful resistance was under Artorius ('King Arthur') who managed to establish an uneasy peace in the south and west. The Anglo-Saxons established seven kingdoms (Northumbria, Mercia, East Anglia, Kent, Essex, Sussex and Wessex) in an area which comprises the present England. They called the dispossessed Britons *wealas*, meaning 'foreigners', from which we get the word *Welsh*.

The native Britons were overcome by the invaders, a fact which shows in the two languages: very few Celtic words appear in English. Old English has only about a dozen words from Celtic. *Crag* and *tor* (rock) and *combe* (valley) are borrowings.

Some river names are Celtic. Avon is the same as the Welsh *Afon* - river. *Lindum Colonia* became Lincoln, partly derived from the Welsh *llyn* - lake. Dubris - after *dwfr* or *d[r* in Welsh - became Dover.

The surprising thing is that the language did not die out altogether. Gaelic continues to be spoken in parts of Western Ireland and the North-West Highlands and Islands of Scotland, but certainly not as extensively as the amount of Welsh which is today spoken in Wales. Despite its being the first to be dominated, and its proximity to English-speakers, Welsh in Wales has survived.

One of the most important reasons for this has been the great pride the Welsh nation possesses for its language and culture. It possesses an unusually high regard for matters of the spirit; poetry, recitation, song and community. In medieval times, the bard was one of the most important members of a nobleman's household. He would recount in verse the battles and heroic deeds of the ancestors. As a scholar, he would be expected to know the language in detail. The bards wrote handbooks to preserve the integrity of the language; some compiled dictionaries. However, because of social changes, by the sixteenth century the order of bards was dying out; patronage decreased. The old Welsh aristocracy, with its medieval tradition of paternalism and service, was past. It was replaced by rich, often English, land-owners, who owned large estates but had no sense of tradition.

Religion kept the language alive. The Bible (under the support of the Tudor Queen Elizabeth 1st) was translated by William Morgan, in an extraordinary feat of scholarship, language skill and determination, in the village of Llanrhaiadr-ym-Mochnant, in the Berwyn hills, between Llangollen and Oswestry. It was published in 1588, and like the King James Bible of 1611, is regarded as a masterpiece of language beauty.

Then came the religious revivals of the eighteenth century. The natural bent of the Welsh towards sharing song and words found an outlet, even if piety in it replaced exuberance. Ministers incanted in Welsh, and people met in discussion groups. The book trade flourished, publishing Bibles and explanations, and there is still today a proliferation of publishers and printers in small towns.

The idea of scholarship and poetry unconnected with the English traditions of position and universities exists in Wales; poetry and the common man have always been together; there is an elitism of talent, not of material position. The need for education came out of underprivilege, the lack of the English system of a higher social caste and its private schools. One interesting event happened in 1846 - Brad y Llyfrau Gleision (The Treason of the Blue Books). In 184

4

a report was published, written by Englishmen, describing the Welsh as being ignorant, illiterate and uncouth - an impression gained probably because most of the population was monoglot Welsh. This bitterly stung the pride of the Welsh. Evening classes started up; religious meetings proliferated. Schools were created, and Wales had a general popular Grammar School system before England. In 1871 the University of Wales was founded with the establishing of University College, Aberystwyth, created through public subscription.

The National Eisteddfod continues today, meeting in north and south Wales in alternate years. The International Eisteddfod in early July in Llangollen has achieved world fame as a centre for folk dance and song excellence. The competitive meeting is centuries old in the Welsh tradition. Socially, it echoes back into small groups gathering in mostly rural areas for an evening of merriment - the Noson Lawen. The dancing and making of poetry was sometimes spontaneous; poems made up on the spot about current affairs and people. Writing of formal verse and winning prizes in the National Eisteddfod, in the last two centuries, has been an activity accompanied by pride, fame and reward.

Today Welsh is holding its own. Although it has been still migrating westwards, it is spoken with pride and vigour by young and old. The streets of Llangefni, Porthmadog, Lampeter and Carmarthen are full of the musical echoes of an ancient and beautiful tongue.

It is hoped that this little booklet will help the visitor to Wales gain an insight into this tough survivor of a language. It describes very broadly the rules of grammar, but greater emphasis has been placed on gaining the use of phrases, and acquiring a useful vocabulary. The words in the vocabulary section can be used with Welsh-speakers who can confirm their pronunciation, and how they are used. There are text-books available from bookshops for those who want to continue their study, and the purchase of a dictionary is recommended.

Speaking Welsh is similar in sound to speaking Spanish or Russian. The sounds are made positively and with vigour: some by blowing outwards. The ch is made by compressing air through the back of the throat (exactly as the Scottish loch). The ll is made by placing the tip of the tongue against the front top of the mouth and blowing air beneath it to one side. Many Welsh place names begin with Llan, so lisen to how Welsh speakers say it and copy them. Do not hesitate to ask Welsh speakers to help you with pronunciation; they will be pleased.

The Welsh alphabet is as follows: A B C CH D DD E F FF G NG H I J L LL M N O P PH R RH S T TH U W Y. Pronunciations are generally phonetic, so when the sounds of the above are mastered, you simply put them together in word order to pronounce the word. The following is a general guide. Consonants. b,d,h,j,l,m,n,p,s,t are sounded as in English. But the following are distinct: c is hard, as in 'cat'; ch, a distinct Welsh sound, see above; dd, tip of the tongue against the top teeth, as in 'them'; f, soft, as in 'vessel'; ff, bottom lip against top teeth, as in 'funnel'; g, as in 'go'; ng, as in 'bring'; ll, see above - and practise! r, a vigorous sound as in 'ringing'; rh, the r followed by a chesty outward blow which is the h, as in 'who'; th as in 'thick'; Vowels: a, the sound of sheep baaaing; e, watch this one, it isn't quite the English e as in eating, it's the sound you make when you havn't quite heard someone, 'eh...eh...'; i as in 'Ee bah gum'; o as in middle of 'call'; w as in 'coo'; u, here the mouth is made into a funnel at the front, and there is no English equivalent; y, as in up.

We hope you will enjoy - and speak - Welsh!   J.I.J.

GRAMMAR

THE ALPHABET

Welsh is a phonetic language, which means that every letter is always pronounced the same way. The only variation is in the amount of stress given to different words. The exceptions to this rule are (a) the letter Y which can be pronounced either 'clear' or 'obscure'; and (b) when the letter S is followed by an I - this forms the 'sh' sound in Welsh. If you practice the sound of every letter, it will enable you to read Welsh fairly easily in a short time, even though you have no idea of the meaning!

The Welsh alphabet has 28 letters as opposed to 26 in the English language. The letters j, k, q, v, x and z are omitted from the Welsh, although j has been used in recent times owing to the absorption of some English words e.g. *garej* for garage, and of course in that most Welsh of surnames, *Jones*. There are an additional 8 letters: ch, dd, ff, ll, ng, ph, rh, th. If you advance sufficiently to be able to do Welsh cross-words, these count as a single letter and go into one square!

Below is the English approximation of the pronounciation of each letter.

a : either long as in *part* or short as in *hat*
b : as in *boat*
c : always hard as in *cart*
ch : no English equivalent, but the same sound as the Scottish loch or the German Bach
d : as in *door*
dd : as *th* in they, *that*
e : either long as in *pale* or short as in *well*
f : as *v* in *wave*
ff : as *f* in *force* or *ff* in *effort*
g : always hard as in *glove, give*
ng : as *ng* in *sing, bring*
h : as in *horse*, never aspirate
i : mostly long as in *need* but sometimes short as in *win*
l : as in *long*
ll : no English equivalent. Place the tip of the tongue against the top front teeth and emit a sharp burst of air without making a noise in the throat
m : as in *man*
n : as in *nail*
o : either long as in *door* or short as in *hop*
p : as in *paper*
ph : as in *pharmacy* or *f* in *front*
r : slightly rolled, *red, robin*
rh : combine the *r* with the *h*, i.e. say both letters quickly
s : as in *sort*
t : as in *tree*
th : as in *thorn, thought*
u : in South Wales this is pronounced as *ee* in *weed* but in North Wales it is more like the *i* in *win*
w : either long as *oo* in school or short as *oo* in look

y : the clear sound is the same as for the letter *u* above; the obscure sound is as the *u* in under, upset. To help your reading, the clear *y* will have ŷ above it (ŷ) and the obscure *y* will have ÿ above it (ÿ) in words used in the text.

VOWELS AND DIPHTHONGS

Welsh has more vowels than English. They are: a, e, i, o, u, w, y. Although there are no diphthongs in Welsh as there are in English, you will often find two vowels placed together. Just remember that the language is phonetic, and that each vowel has to be pronouned separately though smoothly. Generally the stress falls on the first vowel. A few examples to practise are: *cae* (field); *tai* (houses); *cei* (quay); *neu* (or); *cŷw* (chick); *llew* (lion); *oen* (lamb); *uwd* (porridge).

Even more complicated for the non-Welsh speaker is where there are three vowels following each other as in *gloÿw* (bright, shiny), but fortunately these are not very common. If you follow the basic rule of pronouncing each vowel separately you cannot go far wrong.

STRESS

In multisyllabic words, the stress normally falls on the last syllable but one. There are a few exceptions such as mwŷnháu (enjoy) and Caerdydd (Cardiff) where the stress falls on the last syllable. Practise saying these words:
edrŷch (look); *árian* (silver/money); *gobaith* (hope); *blodau* (flowers); *ceffÿlau* (horses); *cérdded* (walk); *traddodiad* (tradition); *gorlléwin* (west); *ménŷn* (butter); *báchgen* (boy); *géneth* (girl); *llÿwodraeth* (government).

MUTATIONS

One aspect of learning Welsh that could be daunting is the use of mutations. These are governed by strict rules as to when a consonant changes to another consonant at the beginning of the word. Most Welsh speakers are unaware of any 'rules' - it comes naturally with familiarity with the language. The ear tells them whether a consonant should mutate or not. But do not let this worry you. You will be perfectly understood if you say the original form of the word. Below is a table of which consonants change and what they change to.

consonant	original form of word	soft mutation	nasal mutation	aspirant mutation
p	pen (head)	ei ben (his)	fÿ mhen (my)	ei phen (her)
t	trwÿn (nose)	ei drwÿn	fÿ nhrwÿn	ei thrwÿn
c	corff (body)	ei gorff	fÿ nghorff	ei chorff
b	bawd (thumb)	ei fawd	fÿ mawd	ei bawd
d	dant (tooth)	ei ddant	fÿ nant	ei dant
g	gwallt (hair)	ei wallt	fÿ ngwallt	ei gwallt
ll	llaw (hand)	ei law	fÿ llaw	ei llaw
m	migwrn (wrist)	ei figwrn	fÿ migwrn	ei migwrn
rh	rhaff (rope)	ei raff	fÿ rhaff	ei rhaff

The rules governing mutations are far too complex to be discussed here. They would only confuse the beginner. The purpose of including the table is to illustrate the way mutations are used, and also so that you will realize that when reading or listening to Welsh, there will be minor changes in the form of certain words. You will be able to work backwards to the original, and not think that you have encountered a strange new word. In the text there will be sentences that contain words where a mutation has taken place. The first letter of these words will be printed in italics.

SIMPLE GREETINGS AND PHRASES

Now that you have gone through the groundwork of letters, their sounds and general pronounciation, you can learn some of the following phrases. They are very simple and are concerned with everyday requests and politenesses.

Bore da	Good morning
P'nawn da	Good afternoon
Nos da	Good night
Diolch	Thanks
Diolch ÿn *f*awr	Thank you very much
Dim diolch	No thank you
Os gwelwch ÿn *dd*a	Please (though *plis* is often used)
Sut rÿdych chi?	How are you?
Iawn, diolch	Fine, thank you
Sut dÿwÿdd yw hi?	What's the weather like?
Mae hi'n braf	It's fine (hot)
Mae hi'n bwrw glaw	It's raining
Mae hi'n oer	It's cold
Mae hi'n wÿntog	It's windy
Mae hi'n *b*oeth	It's hot
Mae hi'n heulog	It's sunny
Eisteddwch i lawr	Sit down
Mae'n ddrwg gen i	Sorry
Rÿdw i'n siarad Cÿmraeg	I speak Welsh
Dÿdw i ddim ÿn siarad Cymraeg	I do not speak Welsh
Siaradwch ÿn araf os gwelwch ÿn dda	Speak more slowly, please
Iechÿd da	Good health (Cheers)
Da boch chi/Hwyl	Goodbye/So long
Fÿ enw ÿw ...	My name is ...
Beth ÿw eich enw?	What's your name?

DAYS OF THE WEEK	DYDDIAU'R WYTHNOS
Sunday	Dÿdd Sul
Monday	Dÿdd Llun
Tuesday	Dÿdd Mawrth
Wednesday	Dÿdd Mercher
Thursday	Dÿdd Iau
Friday	Dÿdd Gwener
Saturday	Dÿdd Sadwrn

MONTHS OF THE YEAR	MISOEDD Y FLWYDDYN
January	Ionawr
February	Chwefror
March	Mawrth
April	Ebrill
May	Mai
June	Mehefin
July	Gorffennaf
August	Awst
September	Medi
October	Hỹdref
November	Tachwedd
December	Rhagfỹr

SEASONS	TYMHORAU
Spring	Gwanwyn
Summer	Haf
Autumn	Hỹdref
Winter	Gaeaf

COUNTING - CYFRIF

After the figures 1-12, there are two forms of counting in Welsh. The older form used to go in multiples of twenties for large figures. It could best be described by visualising Roman numerals, e.g. the way ten (X) plus five (V) makes fifteen. Thus in Welsh fourteen would be pedwar ar ddeg (four on ten), and nineteen would be *pedwar ar bỹmtheg* (four on five on ten). In everyday language the simpler system below is used.

1	un (m/f)	16	un deg chwech
2	dau (m), dwỹ (f)	17	un deg saith
3	tri (m), tair (f)	18	un deg wỹth
4	pedwar (m), pedair (f)	19	un deg naw
5	pump	20	dau *dd*eg
6	chwech	21	dau *dd*eg un
7	saith	30	tri deg
8	wỹth	31	tri deg un
9	naw	40	pedwar deg
10	deg	50	pum deg
11	un deg un	100	cant
12	un deg dau (dwy f)	200	dau *g*ant
13	un deg tri (tair f)	300	tri *ch*ant
14	un deg pedwar (pedair f)	1,000	mil
15	un deg pump	2,000	dau *f*il
		1,000,000	miliwn

GENDER OF NOUNS

As in French, all nouns in Welsh are classified either as masculine or feminine. It is easy to cope with living creatures such as *buwch* (cow) and *tarw* (bull), but inanimate objects and

abstract nouns may cause problems. There is no easy way out. The only way to cope is **
learning words from a dictionary and memorising their gender at the same time. To help yo
remember it may be useful to do a little exercise with each word you learn, as follows:

Masculine nouns	Feminine nouns
ў ...... hwn (this ......)	ў ...... hon (this ......)*

Again, if you make a mistake in gender, you will still be understood. It just sounds odd to t
Welshman.

THE DEFINITE ARTICLE

The word 'the' may be expressed in three different ways. They are:

ў — comes when the following word begins with a consonant, e.g. *y llÿfr* (the book)

ÿr — comes when the following word begins with a vowel or h, e.g. *yr wÿ* (the egg); *yr*
  halen (the salt)

'r — comes when the preceding word ends in a vowel, e.g. *tua'r ÿsgol* (towards the
  school); *gyda'r ferch* (with the girl)

THE INDEFINITE ARTICLE (a/an/any/some)

There is no indefinite article in Welsh. The noun is used in its own, e.g.:

Mae cacen ar ÿ bwrdd	There is a cake on the table
Oes gennÿch chi lÿfrau?	Have you any books?
Mae llÿfrau ar ÿ silff	There are some books on the shelf
Blodÿn tlws	A pretty flower

ˉhe adjective follows the noun in almost every case. The exceptions, notably *hen* (old), are
and need not worry you.

ci bach (little/small dog)   ceffyl mawr (big/large horse)
car coch (red car)   dillad newydd (new clothes)

N.B. - A mutation of the first consonant will often occur in the feminine form after *y*.

RBS

ˉrb conjugations in Welsh are as complicated as conjugations in Latin, and as numerous.
ⁱain the beginner need not sit down and learn all the various forms. Spoken Welsh, which is
ⁱat we are mainly concerned with here, uses very few different tenses and verb-endings.
ⁱere is also a movement away from the formal and somewhat archaic use of verb endings in
tten Welsh. You will notice the various endings in the text; this is a more natural way of
rning them. The most useful verb is *bod*, to be. It is declined below in the present tense. It
ⁱn irregular verb.

Rydw i - I am   Rŷdŷm ni - We are
Rwŷt ti - you (familiar) are   Rŷdŷch chi - You (plural/polite) are
Mae ef - he is   Mae nhw - They are
Mae hi - she is

B. - As in many other European languages, there is a familiar and polite form of the singu-
'you'. Unless you know a person very well indeed, or the person is part of the family, you
ⁱuld use the polite plural form.

NTENCE CONSTRUCTION

The sentence usually begins with the verb:

Mae Iolo ŷn ŷ dref (Iolo is in the town)

already mentioned, the adjective follows the noun:

Mae Iolo ŷn ŷ dref *fawr* (Iolo is in the large town)

ⁱen you have learnt the verb 'to be' you can form very simple sentences quite easily. Use
ⁱ basic formula of:

Mae ...... ŷn ŷ ...... (There is/are ...... in the ......)

d insert either a proper name or a noun where appropriate. For example:

Mae Huw ŷn ŷ siop   Huw is in the shop
Mae siwgr ŷn ŷ siop   There is sugar in the shop
Mae cath ar ŷ mat   There is a cat on the mat
Mae gwartheg ŷn ŷ cae   There are cows in the field
Mae mam wrth ŷ drws   Mother is by the door

Practise as many of these as you can think of, using the vocabulary for nouns. You should
ⁱactise both writing and saying them out loud, building up your ability so that you can think
words and say them immediately. You can also use the other forms of the verb 'to be', e.g.

Rŷdw i yn ŷr ysgol	I am in the school
Mae hi yn ŷ ty	She is in the house
Mae ef yn ŷ llŷfrgell	He is in the library
Rŷdym ni *ar* ŷ llawr	We are *on* the floor
Rŷdych chi *dan* ŷr ambarel	You are *under* the umbrella
Mae nhw *wrth* ŷ parc	They are *by* the park

Using the above formula, you can try ending the sentence with an adjective:

Rŷdw i'n dal	I am tall
Mae hi'n dlws	She is pretty
Mae ef yn ddrwg	He is naughty/bad
Rŷdym ni'n oer	We are cold
Rŷdych chi'n wlyb	You are wet
Mae nhw'n boeth	They are hot

Note that when one word ends with a vowel and the following word begins with a vowel, is normal to drop the second vowel and insert an apostrophe. This is just as in English, when 'It is' is often said as 'It's'. Pronounciation is easier and your speech flows more smoothl Another point to remember here is that there is no such word as 'it' in the Welsh language. 'I is always a he or a she, and therefore you must use ef or hi depending on the gender of th subject. Thus weather is feminine in Welsh (tŷwydd) and so you say:

Mae hi'n braf for It is fine. But more of this later.

We can now progress to substituting another verb for 'to be'. In Welsh when using th present tense of any doing verb we merely stick the verb-noun on to the end of the sentenc which begins with 'I am ...' etc. There is no such ending as the 'ing' in walking, talk-ing, sai ing that you find in English. Study and learn the following examples, then make up your own

Rŷdw i'n cerdded	I am walking
Rŷdw i'n siarad	I am talking
Rŷdw i'n rhedeg	I am running
Mae ef yn hwylio	He is sailing
Mae hi'n marchogaeth	She is riding
Rŷdym ni'n dringo	We are climbing
Rŷdych chi'n nofio	You are swimming
Mae nhw'n cŷsgu	They are sleeping

We have now gone over the simple sentence forms. Firstly we combined the verb 'to be with nouns. Secondly we used 'to be' with adjectives, and lastly we used 'to be' with verb nouns. Once you have mastered these three forms, it is easy to construct sentences whic contain all the elements. We can start off with an example used above:

1.   Rŷdw i'n cerdded
     Rŷdw i'n cerdded ar ŷ mŷnydd
     Rŷdw i'n cerdded ar ŷ mŷnydd uchel
     Rŷdw i'n cerdded yn gŷflym ar ŷ mŷnydd uchel

I am walking
I am walking on the mountain
I am walking on the high mountain
I am walking quickly on the high mountian

2. Mae ef ÿn hwÿlio
    Mae ef ÿn hwÿlio ar ÿ mor
    Mae ef ÿn hwÿlio mewn cwch ar ÿ mor
    Mae ef ÿn hwÿlio mewn cwch coch ar ÿ mor
    Mae ef ÿn hwÿlio mewn cwch coch ar ÿ mor mawr

    He is sailing
    He is sailing on the sea
    He is sailing in a boat on the sea
    He is sailing in a red boat on the sea
    He is sailing in a red boat on the open sea

13

Now you construct your own sentences using the following combinations:

Mae hi'n marchogaeth; ceffÿl; du; yn gÿflÿm.
She is riding; horse; black; quickly/fast.

Rÿdÿm ni'n dringo; clogwÿn; perÿglus; gofalus
We are climbing; cliff; dangerous; carefully

Rÿdÿch chi'n nofio; dwr; dwfn; crÿf.
You are swimming; water; deep; strongly

Mae nhw'n cÿsgu; gwelÿ; plu; trwm.
They are sleeping; bed; feather; heavily.

Now you can go on to form your own long sentences. But to help you to know if you hav
the correct construction, below are the fullest forms of the above combinations.

Mae hi'n marchogaeth ÿn gÿflÿm ar ÿ ceffÿl du.
She is riding fast on the black horse.

Rÿdÿm ni'n dringo'n ofalus ar ÿ clogwÿn perÿglus.
We are climbing carefully on the dangerous cliff.

Rÿdych chi'n nofio'n gryf ÿn ÿ dwr dwfn.
You are swimming strongly in the deep water.

Mae nhw'n cÿsgu'n drwm ÿn ÿ gwelÿ plu.
They are sleeping heavily in the feather bed.

THE NEGATIVE

You will often need to use the negative form in your conversation. This is quite simp
done. An easy way to remember is that you substitute the letter D for the letter R and ad
ddim as shown below:

Rÿdw i	becomes	Dÿdw i ddim
Rÿdÿm ni	becomes	Dÿdÿm ni ddim
Rÿdÿch chi	becomes	Dÿdÿch chi ddim

He, she and they are slightly different.

Mae ef/hi	becomes	Dyw ef/hi ddim
Maent hwÿ	becomes	Dÿdÿn nhw ddim

Sentences are formed as follows:

Dÿdw i ddim ÿn cerdded	I am not walking
Dyw ef ddim ÿn eistedd	He is not sitting
Dyw hi ddim ÿn siarad	She is not talking

14

Dŷdŷm ni ddim ŷn bwŷta	We are not eating
Dŷdŷch chi ddim ŷn gwrando	You are not listening
Dŷdŷn nhw ddim ŷn edrŷch	They are not looking

PAST TENSE

Another form that often pops up in conversation is the past tense. In this booklet we will only deal with the simple form of the past tense. This involves changing one word of a sentence:

Rŷdw i ŷn bwŷta (I am eating) becomes Rŷdw i wedi bwŷta (I have eaten)
Rŷdŷm ni ŷn dod (We are coming) becomes Rŷdŷm ni wedi dod (We have come)

You can carry on changing sentences from present to past by substituting *wedi* for ŷn. Thus:

Rŷd^ch chi *wedi* cyrraedd	You have arrived
Mae nhw *wedi* cerdded	They have walked
Mae'r ceffŷl *wedi* carlamu	The horse has galloped
Mae John *wedi* mynd	John has gone

And the negative:

Dŷdi John ddim wedi mŷnd	John has not gone
Dŷdi'r ceffŷl ddim wedi carlamu	The horse has not galloped
Dŷdyn nhw ddim wedi cerdded	They have not walked
Dŷdw i ddim wedi bwŷta	I have not eaten

Now change these above examples back into the present tense. It will be good practice for you.

TIME

By now you will have learned points of grammar. To give you a break we will deal with telling the time.

The units of time in Welsh are as follows:

second/s	—	eiliad/au	morning/s —	bore/au
minute/s	—	munud/au	afternoon/s —	p'nawn/iau
hour/s	—	awr, pl. oriau	yesterday —	ddoe
day/s	—	dŷdd/iau; diwrnod	today —	heddiw
week/s	—	wŷthnos/au	tomorrow —	ŷforŷ
fortnight	—	pŷthefnos	this year —	eleni
month/s	—	mis/oedd	century/ies —	canrif/oedd
year/s	—	blwŷddŷn, blynyddoedd	age/s —	oes/oedd

If you want to find out the time you say:

Faint o'r gloch ŷw hi os gwelwch ŷn dda?

The reply could be:

15

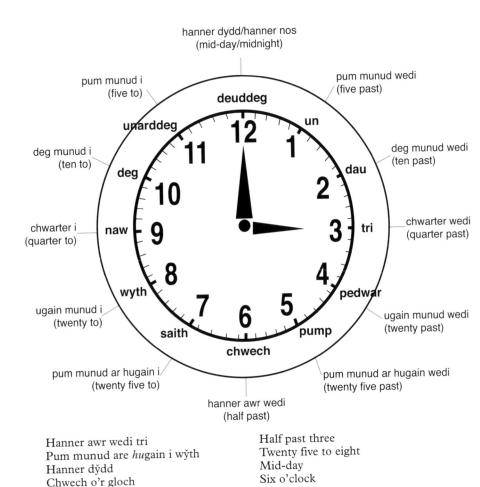

Hanner awr wedi tri	Half past three
Pum munud are *hu*gain i wŷth	Twenty five to eight
Hanner dŷdd	Mid-day
Chwech o'r gloch	Six o'clock

In Welsh you never find the shortened version, e.g. three-fifteen or seven-thirty five. The number of minutes past or the hour come first, then the hour itself.

You would give the date in Welsh as follows:

Dŷdd Mawrth, Hŷdref pumed, mil naw cant saith deg chwech.
 Tuesday, October 5, 1976.
Dŷdd Sadwrn, Mai degfed, mil naw cant wŷth deg.
 Saturday, May 10, 1980.

Note that the year translates literally into one thousand nine hundred and eighty.

QUESTIONS AND ANSWERS

The formation of a question follows a single pattern which will be demonstrated below

Answering in the affirmative or negative, however, might pose a few problems. It is easy enough in English to state merely 'yes' or 'no'. In Welsh, though, there are many forms, often using the verb used in the question. Thus:

Ydi'r tecell ar ÿ tan?   Is the kettle on the fire?
Ydi, mae'r tecell ar ÿ tan?   Yes (literally It is), the kettle is on
                                                          the fire.

In everyday use, you can dispense with most of the reply and just use the *Ydi*.

The negative form is *Nag ÿdi*.
Nag ÿdi, dÿw'r tecell ddim ar ÿ tan.

Again practise the formula:

Ydi'r ci wrth ÿ drws?   Is the dog by the door?
Ydi/Nag ÿdi   Yes/No
Ydi'r llÿfr ar ÿ bwrdd?   Is the book on the table?
Ydi/Nag ÿdi
Ydi'r ffenestr ar agor?   Is the window open?
Ydi/Nag ÿdi

If the subject of the question is in the plural, then we use the form *ÿdyn/nag ÿdyn*

Ydi'r ieir ÿn dodwy w^au?   Are the hens laying eggs?
Ydyn/nag ÿdÿn

17

Ydi'r dail ẙn disgẙn?	Are the leaves falling?
Ydyn/nag ẙdẙn	
Ydi'r trenau ẙn rhedeg?	Are the trains running?
Ydẙn/nag ẙdẙn	

If you are using personal pronouns, then you use the appropriate form of the verb 'to be'.

Yd^ch chi'n barod?	Are you ready?
Ydw/nag ẙdw	(Remember that you use the polite and plural form for 'you', so your reply would depend on whether you were a group or an individual)
Ydy hi'n mẙnd gartref?	Is she going home?
Ydi/nag ẙdi	
Ydw i'n cael afal?	Am I having an apple
Ydych/nag ẙdẙch	
Ydym ni'n blant da?	Are we good children
Ydych/nag ẙdẙch	

WHY? PAM?

When you wish to find out why, the easiest way is to insert Pam at the beginning of the sentence.

Mae'r tren ẙn hwẙr	The train is late
Pam mae'r tren ẙn hwẙr?	Why is the train late?
Mae'r ci ẙn cyfarth	The dog is barking
Pam mae'r ci ẙn cyfarth?	Why is the dog barking?
Rẙdẙch chi'n chwerthin	You are laughing
Pam rẙdẙch chi'n chwerthin?	Why are you laughing?

The usual reply would begin with the words *Am fod* (because). Thus:

Pam mae'r tren ẙn hwẙr?	Why is the train late?
Am fod damwain wedi digwẙdd	Because there has been an accident

WHERE? BLE?

Again you insert *Ble* in front of *mae*.

Ble mae'r car?	Where is the car?
Ble mae'r siopau?	Where are the shops?

In the reply you can either repeat the question without the *Ble* and add where it is:

Ble mae'r plant?	Where are the children?
Mae'r plant are lan ẙ mor	The children are by the seaside

Or you can use the shortened version:

| Ar lan ỹ mor | By the seaside |
| Yn ỹ dref | In the town |

IS/ARE THERE? OES?

In Welsh, the one word *oes* is used for the singular and the plural. No other part of the verb is necessary.

Oes plant are lan ỹ mor?	Are there children by the seaside?
Oes te ỹn ỹ tebot?	Is there tea in the teapot?
Oes lle ar ỹ bws?	Is there room on the bus?

The reply is quite simple. Yes is *oes* and no is *nagoes*.

Oes eira ar ỹ mỹnỹdd?	Is there snow on the mountain?
Oes, mae eira ar ỹ mỹnỹdd.	Yes, there is snow on the mountain.
Oes ceffỹlau ỹn ỹ cae?	Are there horses in the field?
Oes/nagoes	Yes/No

WHO? PWY?

Pwỹ is always followed by *sỹdd*, very rarely by *mae*.

Pwỹ sỹdd ỹn ỹr ardd?	Who is in the garden?
John sỹdd ỹn ỹr ardd.	John is in the garden.
Pwy sỹdd eiddo'r tỹ ỹna?	Who owns that house?
Mr. Huws sydd eiddo'r tỹ ỹna.	Mr. Hughes owns that house.
Pwy sỹ'n eistedd ar ỹ fainc?	Who is sitting on the bench?
Cardotỹn sy'n eistedd ar ỹ fainc.	A tramp is sitting on the bench.

Note that in the last example the *sỹdd* has been changed to *sỹ'*. This is for the convenience of the speaker, for *sỹ'* is often easier to pronounce than *sỹdd*.

WHAT? BETH?

Again *beth* combines with *sỹdd* (or *sỹ'*) to form the question.

| Beth sydd ỹn ỹ siop? | What is in the shop? |
| Dodrefn sỹdd ỹn ỹ siop? | There is furniture in the shop. |

Note that the object of the answer comes first in the sentence.

Beth sy'n disgỹn?	What is falling?
Glaw sy'n disgỹn.	Rain is falling.
Beth sy'n bod?	What's the matter?
Dim bỹd.	Nothing.

WHEN? PRYD?

Pryd is coupled with *mae*.

| Pryd mae'r tren ỹn cỹrraedd? | When is the train arriving? |

Saith o'r gloch.	Seven o'clock.
Pryd mae amser agor?	When is opening time?
Hanner awr wedi pump.	Five thirty.

HOW MANY? FAINT O/SAWL?

In North Wales most people use the form *Faint o*, but in the South they use *Sawl*. It doesn matter which you use - they are universally understood.

Faint o wŷau sydd ŷn ŷ fasged?	How many eggs are there in the basket?
Sawl wŷ sŷdd ŷn ŷ fasged?	do. do.
Dwsin a hanner.	A dozen and a half.

If you use the first example, you must know the plural form of the noun. If you use the secor way, the singular of the noun follows. Thus it might well be easier for you to use Sawl.

USEFUL PHRASES

The following section gives you some useful phrases in various situations you might er counter on your holidays. Firstly we shall deal with some aspects of travelling in Wales.

Asking the way	*Gofyn y ffordd*
Where is the beach please?	Ble mae'r traeth os gwelwch ŷn dda?
(cinema, garage, hotel, shop, restaurant, church, etc.)	(sinema, garej, gwestŷ, siop, bwŷdŷ, eglwŷs, etc.)
How do we get to Caernarfon?	Sut mae mŷnd i Gaernarfon?

ake the A55 to Bangor then follow the signs.	Cÿmerwch yr A55 i Fangor ÿna dilÿnwch ÿr arwÿddion.
Vhich is the best road to Abersoch?	Pa un ÿw'r ffordd orau i Abersoch?
Through Pwllheli and Llanbedrog.	Drwÿ Pwllheli a Llanbedrog.
Iow far is it to Aberystwyth?	Faint o ffordd sydd ÿna i Aberÿstw^th?
Thirty miles.	Deg milltir ar hugain.
Vhere is the butcher's shop?	Ble mae siop ÿ cigÿdd?
In the high street.	Yn ÿ strÿd fawr.
Vhere is the railway station?	Ble mae'r orsaf rheilffÿrdd?
It is the second street on your left.	Mae ÿn ÿr ail strÿd ar ÿ chwith.
Are there any public conveniences in the town?	Oes cÿfleusterau cÿhoeddus ÿn ÿ dref?
Yes, take the first turning left and the second on the right.	Oes, cÿmerwch ÿ troead cÿntaf ar ÿ chwith a'r ail ar ÿ dde.
Is this the way to .....?	Ai dÿma'r ffordd i .....?
Iow long will it take to get to .....?	Faint o amser a gÿmerith i fÿnd i ...?
Is it far?	Ydi o'n bell?
Is it a good road?	Ydi hi'n ffordd dda?

In the Garage	Yn y Garej
Can I have five gallons of petrol please?	Ga'i bump galwÿn o betrol os gwelwch ÿn dda?
And a pint of oil - any 20/50 will do.	A pheint o olew - fe wnaiff unrhÿw 20/50 ÿ tro.
Have you an air line?	Oes lein wynt gennÿch?
I want to check the air in my tyres.	Rydw i eisiau mesur ÿ gwynt ÿn ÿ teiars.
Can you clean the windscreen please?	Fedrwch chi lanhau'r ffenestr os gwelwch ÿn dda.
Do you sell sweets/maps here?	Ydych chi'n gwerthu melÿsion/mapiau ÿma?
Can you fill the radiator with water please?	Fedrwch chi lenwi'r radiator a dwr os gwelwch ÿn dda?
And the battery too.	A'r batri hefÿd.
I've run out of petrol.	Rwÿf wedi rhedeg allan o betrol.
Can I have a gallon can of petrol please?	Ga'i gan galwÿn o betrol os gwelwch ÿn dda?
Is there a mechanic here?	Oes peiriannÿdd ÿma?
My car has broken down.	Mae fÿ nghar wedi torri i lawr.
Can you tow it to the garage?	Fedrwch chi ei dÿnnu i'r garej?
Can you repair it?	Fedrwch chi ei drwsio?
The car won't start.	Wnaiff ÿ car ddim cÿchwÿn.
My fan belt has broken.	Mae belt ÿ ffan wedi torri.
I want a new one.	Rÿdw i eisiau un newÿdd.
The engine is over-heating.	Mae'r injan ÿn poethi.
The battery is flat.	Mae'r batri ÿn fflat.
The radiator is leaking.	Mae'r radiator ÿn gollwng dwr.
Can you look at the brakes?	Fedrwch chi edrych ar ÿ brecs?
They are not safe.	Dÿdyn nhw ddim ÿn saff.

ACCOMMODATION (HOTELS)

I would like a single room with bathroom for tonight and tomorrow, please.	Rÿdw i eisiau ÿstafell senlg gÿda 'stafell molchi am heno a nos ÿforÿ os gwelwch ÿn dda.
Sorry, we are fully booked for the next two weeks.	Mae'n *dd*rwg gen i ond mae'r gwestÿ'n llawn am ÿ pÿthefnos nesaf.
I have booked one double room for tonight	Rydw i wedi llogi un ÿstafell ddwbl am henc
Will you please sign the register.	*W*newch chi arwÿddo'r cofrestr os gwelwch ÿn dda.
Do you have reduced rates for children?	Oes prisiau rhatach i *b*lant?
In the off season but not in the busy season.	Oes, ÿn ÿ tymor distaw, ond dim ÿn ÿ tÿmor prÿsur.
Can we have a cot for the baby?	Gawn ni *g*ot i'r babi?
Are dogs allowed?	Gaiff cwn *dd*od i mewn?
Not in the public rooms.	*Dd*im i'r 'stafelloedd cÿhoeddus.
We would like to have breakfast in our room.	Hoffwn gael ein brecwast ÿn ein 'stafell.
I would like a newspaper every morning.	Hoffwn *g*ael papur newydd *b*ob bore.
Is there a lift in the hotel?	Oes esgÿnfa ÿn ÿ gwestÿ?
Is there a television in the room?	Oes teledu ÿn ÿr ÿstafell?
No, we have a television lounge.	Na, mae gennym lolfa *d*eledu.
I want a room overlooking the sea/mountain /lake.	Rÿdw i eisiau 'stafell sÿ'n edrÿch dros ÿ môr /mÿnÿdd/llÿn.
Where is the bathroom/toilet?	Ble mae'r 'stafell molchi/toiled?
Where is the telephone?	Ble mae'r teliffon?
Do you have a swimming pool?	Oes gennÿch chi *b*wll nofio?
Where is the restaurant?	Ble mae'r 'stafell *f*wÿta?
Through the lounge on your right.	*Dr*wÿ'r lolfa ar ÿ llaw dde.
Is breakfast included in the price?	Ydi'r pris ÿn cÿnnwÿs brecwast?
Can I have the bill please?	*Ga*' i'r cÿfrif os gwelwch ÿn *dd*a?
I shall be leaving early tomorrow morning.	Bÿddaf ÿn gadael ÿn fuan bore 'forÿ.
This bill is incorrect.	Mae'r cÿfrif ÿma ÿn anghÿwir.
I want to see the manager.	Rÿdw is eisiau gweld y rheolwr.

CAMPING AND CARAVANS / PEBYLL A CHARAFANNAU

Where is there a caravan/camping site?	Ble mae 'na *f*aes carafannau/pebÿll?
Can we put up our tent in your field, please?	Gawn ni roi ein pabell ÿn eich cae chi, os gwelwch ÿn *dd*a?
What are the daily rates?	Beth yw'r tâl dÿddiol?
How long can we stay?	Am faint gawn ni aros?
Are there any washing facilities on the site?	Oes cÿfleusterau molchi ar ÿ maes?
Are there any toilets on the site?	Oes toiledi ar ÿ maes?
Can we light a fire?	*G*awn ni *g*ÿnna tân?
Is there water nearby?	Oes d[r ÿn ÿmÿl?
Do you sell milk/eggs?	Ydÿch chi'n gwerthu llefrith (llaeth in S. Wales)/wÿau?
Where can we get a bottle of gas?	Ble gawn ni botel o nwy?
Are there any dangerous animals around?	Oes anifeiliaid perÿglus o gwmpas?
Is the ground hard/soft?	A yw'r ddaear ÿn galed/feddal?
Is the ground stony?	A yw'r ddaear ÿn garregog?

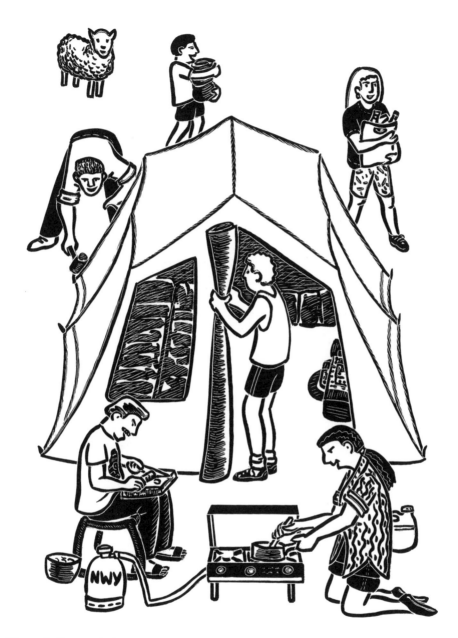

Where shall we park the caravan?
Where shall we put up the tent?
Is there shop on the site?

Ble wnawn ni roi'r garafan?
Ble wnawn ni roi'r babell i fyny"
Oes siop ar ÿ maes?

Dogs must be kept under control.	Rhaid cadw cwn dan reolaeth.
We only have campers.	Dim ond gwesÿllwyr sydd ÿma.
We have no room for touring caravans.	Does dim llê gennym i garafannau teithiol.

| Who is in charge here? | Pwy sy'n gÿfrifol am ÿ lle? |
| I want to speak to the warden. | Rÿdw i eisiau siarad â'r warden. |

| SHOPPING | YN Y SIOPAU |

Having arrived safely at your destination, you will have time to visit the local shops, either for food or for gifts to take home with you.

The first section of phrases will deal with how to ask for things in general. Then there will be a separate section for the various types of shops.

How much is this, please?	Faint ÿw hwn os gwelwch ÿn dda?
Two pounds fifty pence.	Dwÿ bunt a phum deg ceiniog.
It is expensive!	Mae o'n ddrud!
It is cheap!	Mae o'n rhad!
Do you have any .....?	Oes gennÿch chi .....?
I want some ....., please.	Rÿdw i eisiau ..... os gwelwch ÿn dda.
Is it fresh?	Ydi o'n ffres?
Is it made locally?	Ydi o wedi ei wneud ÿn lleol?
Is it made in Wales?	Ydi o wedi ei wneud ÿng Nghÿmru?
I am looking for some	Rÿdw i'n chwilio am .....
How much is the bill?	Faint ÿw'r bil?

WEIGHTS AND MEASURES

ounce	—	owns	two pounds	— dau *bwŷs*
quarter pound	—	chwarter pwŷs	three pounds	— tri *phwŷs*
half pound	—	hanner pwŷs	five pounds	— pum pwŷs
pound	—	pwŷs	ten pounds	— deg pwŷs

inches	—	modfeddi	half dozen	— hanner dwsin
feet	—	troedfeddi	dozen	— dwsin
yards	—	llathenni	two dozen	— dau *dd*wsin
miles	—	milltiroedd		

pint	—	peint	quart	— chwart
half pint	—	hanner peint	gallon	— galwŷn

GROCERS

I want half a pound of butter, please.

How much is the cheese?
Twenty pence a quarter.
Have you got some fresh cream?

SIOP FWYD

Rŷdw i eisiau hanner pwys of *f*enyn, os
  gwelwch yn *dd*a.
*F*aint ŷw'r caws?
Ugain ceiniog ŷ chwarter.
oes hufen ffres gennŷch chi?

tea	— tê	honey	— mêl
coffee	— coffi	salt	— halen
milk	— llefrith/llaeth	pepper	— pupur
sugar	— iwgwr	mustard	— mwstard
eggs	— wŷau	herbs	— perlŷsiau
bacon	— cig mochŷn	currants	— cÿrens
flour	— blawd	custard	— cwstard
wheat flour	— blawd gwenith	cocoa	— coco
oat flour	— blawd ceirch	rice	— reis
cakes	— cacenni/teisenni	soup	— cawl
porridge	— uwd	candles	— canhwÿllau
jam	— jam	yeast	— burum
marmalade	— marmaled	biscuits	— bisgedi
chocolate	— siocled	canned meat	— cig tin
orange juice	— sûdd oren	grapefruit juice	— sûdd grawnffrwyth

GREENGROCERS

A pound of apples please.
Are they grown locally?
Are they ripe?
These are over-ripe.
Are they sweet/sour?
Are they hard/soft?

SIOP FFRWYTHAU

Pwys o afalau os gwelwch yn *dd*a.
Ydŷn nhw'n cael eu tÿfu'n lleol?
Ydŷn nhw'n aeddfed?
Mae'r rhain ŷn or-aeddfed.
Ydŷn nhw'n *f*elÿs/chwerw?
Ydŷn nhw'n *g*aled/feddal?

apples	— afalau	blackberries	— mwyar duon
oranges	— orennau	blackcurrants	— cÿrens duon
bananas	— bananas	red currants	— cÿrens coch
grapes	— grawnwin	gooseberries	— eirin Mair (gwsberis)
grapefruit	— grawnffrw^th	pineapple	— pinafal

plums	—	eirin	melon	—	melwn
pears	—	gellig	peaches	—	eirin gwlanog
nuts	—	cnau	apricots	—	bricŷll
cherries	—	ceirios	strawberries	—	mefus
lemons	—	lemon	raspberries	—	mafon
cress	—	berw	parsnip	—	pannas

otatoes	— tatws	celery	—	helogan
arrots	— moron	leek	—	cenhinen
eas	— pŷs	swede	—	rwden
eans	— ffa	turnip	—	meipen
omatoes	— tomatos	onions	—	nionod (NW)/ winwns (SW)
ttuce	— letŷs			
abbage	— bresŷch	garlic	—	garlleg
auliflower	— blodfresŷch	cucumber	—	cucumber
		watercress	—	berw dŵr

BUTCHERS

Can I have some Welsh lamb, please?

How much would you like?
About three quarters of a pound.
Enough for four people.
Is it from the deep-freeze?
No, it's home killed.
How much per pound is it?

CIGYDD

Ga'i *rŷwfaint* o oen Cŷmreig os gwelwch ŷn dda?
Faint ŷdŷch chi eisiau?
Rhŷw *dri* chwarter pwŷs.
Digon i *bedwar* o *bobl.
Ydi o o'r rhewgell?
Na, mae wedi i *ladd* gartref.
Faint ŷ pwŷs ŷdi o?

eef	— winwns (SW)cig eidion	pork	—	winwns (SW)porc
teak	— winwns (SW)golw^th	bacon	—	cig mochŷn
ump	— tîn	ham	—	ham
illet	— golwŷth	lamb	—	cig oen
ack	— cefn	Welsh lamb	—	oen Cŷmreig
eg	— coes	mutton	—	cig dafad
houlder	— ÿsgwŷdd	chicken	—	cyw iâr
risket	— barwŷden	veal	—	cig llo
ongue	— tafod	duck	—	hwŷaden
rawn	— baeddgig	turkey	—	wrci
ffal	— perfedd	goose	—	gwŷdd
iver	— iau/afu	sausages	—	sosej
eart	— calon	kidney	—	aren

FISHMONGERS

plaice	— lleden	lobster	—	cimwch
od	— (SW)cig eidionpenfras	sole	—	lleden
ake	— (SW)cig eidioncegddu	smoked	—	mygu
erring	— penwaig	salted	—	halltu
nackerel	— mecryll	haddock	—	hadog
hrimps	— berdysa	whiting	—	gwyniad
rawns	— corgimwch	mussels	—	cregyn gleision
rab	— cranc	cockles	—	cocos
		oysters	—	wystrus

SIOP BYSGOD

WELSH CRAFT SHOP

Is this Welsh tapestry material?
Where is the woollen mill?
May I try this on?

SIOP GREFFTAU CYMREIG

Gwlanen *Gŷ*mreig ŷw hwn?
Ble mae'r *f*elin *w*lan?
Ga'i *d*reio hwn arna'i?

What size is it?	Beth ÿw ei faint?
I wear size	Rÿdw i'n gwisgo seis .....
Do you have any other colours?	Oes lliwiau eraill gennÿch?
Is it pure wool?	Ydi hwn o wlân pûr?
Is the mill open to the public?	Ydi'r felin wlân ar agor i'r cyhoedd?
Is this pottery made in Wales?	Ydi'r crochenwaith ÿma wedi ei wneud ÿng Nghÿmru?
What is the name of the potter?	Beth yw enw'r crochennÿdd?
Are there many local craftsmen?	Oes llawer o grefftwÿr lleol?
Have you any lovespoons?	Oes llwÿau caru gennÿch?
Have you a book on lovespoons?	Oes llÿfr ar lwÿau caru gennÿch?
What is the history of the lovespoon?	Beth ÿw hanes ÿ lwÿ garu?
What is the meaning of the symbols?	Beth yw ÿstÿr ÿ sÿmbolau?
I'm looking for a present for my mother/father etc.	Rÿdw i'n chwilio am anrheg i mam/ nhad etc.
I don't want to spend more than a pound.	Dÿdw i ddim eisiau gwario mwÿ na punt.
Have you anything with Wales written on it?	Oes gennÿch chi rÿwbeth gyda Cÿmru arno?
How much is this tapestry bedspread?	Beth yw pris ÿ garthen Gymreig ÿma?

BAKERS

Have you any bara brith⋆?
  (⋆ a Welsh speciality)
Small white loaf, please.

POBYDD

Oes gennÿch chi fara brith?

Torth wen fach, os gwelwch ÿn dda.

Large brown loaf, please.		Torth *fawr frown*, os gwelwch ÿn *dd*a.	
Are the cakes home baked?		Ydi'r cacenni wedi i bobi gartref?	
Is it today's bread?		Bara heddiw ÿdi o?	
Are the cakes filled with fresh cream?		Ydi'r cacenni wedi eu llenwi a hufen ffres?	
What's in the pie?		Beth sydd yn ÿ *b*astai?	

white bread	— bara gwÿn	buns	— bÿns
brown bread	— bara brown	pies	— pastai
cakes	— cacenni/teisenni	tart	— teisen
fruit cake	— cacen ffrw^thau	apple tart	— teisen afal
fresh cream	— hufen ffres	loaf	— torth

CHEMISTS

FFERYLLYDD

soap	— sebon	bandage	— rhwÿmÿn
toothpaste	— pâst dannedd	plaster	— plastr
toothbrush	— brws dannedd	deodorant	— diaroglwr
medicine	— moddion, ffisÿg	shampoo	— golchwr pen
prescription	— cÿfarwÿddÿd	ointment	— eli
disinfectant	— diheintiwr	comb	— crîb
perfume	— perarogl	brush	— brws
drugs	— cÿffuriau	tablets	— tabledi

POST OFFICE

SWYDDFA'R POST

Twenty-six pence stamp please.	Stamp dau *dd*eg chwech os gwelwch ÿn *dd*a.
Twenty-pence stamp please.	Stamp dau *dd*eg os gwellwch ÿn *dd*a.
How much is it to send this?	Faint *fÿ*dd o i ÿrru hwn?
I want to send this letter by registered post.	Rÿdw i eisiau gÿrru hwn gÿda post cofrestredig.
What time does the post go?	Pa brÿd mae'r post ÿn m^nd?
I want to send this first class/second class.	Rÿdw i eisiau gÿrru hwn gÿda'r post cÿntaf/ail *b*ost.
Can I have a postal order for £2.50 please.	Ga'i ordor post am *dd*wÿ *b*unt a *ph*um deg ceiniog os gwelwch ÿn *dd*a.

ENTERTAINMENT

DIDDANION

When on holiday you obviously want to enjoy yourselves and be fully occupied. There are many open air activities you can pursue in Wales as well as a few evening entertainments. Below are listed some activities with the relevant vocabulary. But first we will deal with day to day social encounters.

AT THE PUB

YN Y DAFARN

Good evening.	Noswaith *dd*a.
Can I have a pint of beer, please?	Ga'i *b*eint o *g*wrw os gwelwch ÿn *dd*a?
Two glasses of red/white wine, please?	Dau *w*ÿdr o *w*în coch/gwÿn os gwelwch ÿn *dd*a.
One whisky and ginger and one brandy please.	Un chwisgi a sinsir ac un brandi os gwelwch ÿn *dd*a.
What will you have to drink?	Beth *g*ÿmerwch chi i ÿfed?
Do you serve snacks/meals?	Ydÿch chi'n gwerthu snaciau/prÿdiau bwÿd?

29

| Cheers! | Iechŷd da! |
| Same again, please. | 'Run peth eto os gwelwch ŷn *dd*a. |

Remember that in some areas of Wales, especially the western parts, the pubs are closed c Sundays.

EATING OUT / BWYTA ALLAN

We have reserved a table for four at o'r eight o'clock.	Rŷdŷm wedi llogi bwrdd i bedwar am wŷth gloch.
Can we see the menu please?	Gawn ni *w*eld ŷ fwŷdlen os gwelwch ŷn *dd*a.
What will you have?	Beth *g*ŷmerwch chi?
What do you recommend?	Beth ŷdych chi'n ei argŷmell
Can I have the vegetable soup followed by the Welsh lamb in honey sauce.	*G*a' i'r cawl llŷsiau, ac i *dd*ilŷn ŷr oen Cŷmreig mewn saws mêl.
Can I see the wine list?	*G*a'i weld ŷ rhestr *w*în?
A bottle of number thirty one, please.	Potel rhif tri deg un os gwelwch ŷn *dd*a.
Does the price include vegetables?	Ydi'r prîs yn cŷnnwys llŷsiau?
Can I see the sweet trolley please?	*G*a'i *w*eld ŷ bwrdd melŷsion os gwelwch ŷn *dd*a.
Coffee for four, please.	Coffi i *b*edwar, os gwelwch ŷn *dd*a.
My compliments to the chef.	Fy llongŷfarchiadau i'r cogŷdd.
The food is cold.	Mae'r bwŷd ŷn oer.
This food is inedible.	Mae'r bwŷd yma ŷn anfwŷtadwŷ.
I want to see the manager.	Rŷdw i eisiau gweld ŷ rheolwr.

ON THE BEACH / AR Y TRAETH

Where is there a safe beach for children?	Ble mae 'na *d*raeth diogel i *b*lant?
Can we take the car or do we have to walk?	Allwn ni *f*ŷnd a'r car neu oes rhaid i ni gerdded?
Can I hire a deck chair please?	*G*a'i *l*ogi sedd *g*anfas os gwelwch ŷn *dd*a?
Where can I get some ice cream?	Ble alla'i *g*ael hufen iâ?
Is the beach very crowded?	Ydi'r traeth ŷn *b*oblog iawn?
Where is there a secluded beach?	Ble mae 'na *d*raeth distaw?
We are all going swimming?	Rŷdŷm i gŷd ŷn mŷnd i nofio.
The sea is very cold.	Mae'r môr yn oer iawn.
When is high tide/low tide?	Prŷd mae llanw/trai?
Is the sea going in or out?	Ydi'r môr ŷn dod i mewn neu ŷn mŷnd allan
Is the beach rocky/sandy?	Ydi'r traeth ŷn *g*arregog/dŷwodlŷd?
Are there strong tides here?	Oes llanw crŷf yma?
Where is there a sailing club?	Ble mae 'na *g*lwb hwŷlio?
Is that your boat?	Eich cwch chi ŷw honna?
Do you race your yacht?	Ydŷch chi'n rasio eich c[ch hwŷlio?
Are you a keen yachtsman?	Ydŷch chi'n hwŷliwr brwd?
There's a strong breeze for sailing.	Mae awel crŷf i hwŷlio.
The weather forecast is not good.	Dŷdi rhagolŷgon ŷ tŷwŷdd *dd*im ŷn *dd*a.
There is a storm on the way.	Mae storom ar ei ffordd.
The sea is very calm.	Mae'r môr ŷn *d*awel iawn.
There is a regatta at Aberdaron.	Mae regata ŷn Aberdaron.

| Where do you keep your boat? | Ble rÿdych chi'n cadw eich cwch? |
| Where do you keep your boat over the winter? | Ble rÿdych chi'n cadw eich cwch dros ÿ gaeaf? |

RIDING

Where is there a pony trekking centre?
How many ponies are there?
How many people go out together?

Is there a guide/leader?
Do you go out on the roads?
Do you go out over the mountains?
Do you have quiet horses?
We are beginners.
We are experienced riders.

MARCHOGAETH

Ble mae 'na ganolfan merlota?
Sawl merlŷn sŷdd ŷna?
Faint o bobol fŷdd ŷn mŷnd allan gÿda'i
  gilŷdd?
Oes ŷna arweinŷdd?
Ydŷch chi'n mynd allan ar ÿ ffÿrdd?
Ydŷch chi'n mŷnd allan dros ÿ mÿnÿddoedd
Oes ceffÿlau tawel gennÿch?
Dÿsgwyr ŷdÿm ni.
Rŷdÿm ni ŷn farchogwŷr profiadol.

32

ENWAU PRIODOL

English	Cymraeg	English	Cymraeg
Adam	Adda	Jane	Sian
Agnes	Nest	Janet	Sioned
Alex ander	Alecsander	Jenny	Siani
Alice	Alis	John	Ioan, Sion
Ambrose	Emrys	Julian	Sulien
Andrew	Andreas	Justin	Iestyn
Anita	Enid	Laura	Lowri
Anne	Nan	Lewis	Lewys
Anthony	Antwn	Lloyd	Llwyd
Arnold	Arnallt	Lucy	Lleucu
Bartholomew	Bartholomeus	Luke	Luc
Beatrice	Betris	Lynette	Luned
Bevan	Bifan	Mabel	Mabli
Bridget	Ffraid	Magdalene	Modlen
Catherine	Catrin	Malcolm	Moelcwlwm
Cecil	Seisyllt	Margaret	Marged
Charles	Siarl	Mark	Marc
Christina	Cristin	Mary	Mair
Claire	Clêr	Maud	Mallt
Daniel	Deiniol	Michael	Mihangel
David	Dewi, Dafydd	Molly	Mali
Dave	Dai, Deio	Nicholas	Niclas
Dennis	Dynys	Oliver	Olfyr
Edmund	Edmwnt	Oswald	Oswallt
Edward	Iorwerth	Owen	Owain
Eleanor	Linor	Patrick	Padrig
Ellen	Elin	Paul	Pawl
Emma	Em	Perceval	Peredur
Enoch	Enoc	Peter	Pedr
Evan	Ifan, Ieuan	Philip	Phylip
Eve	Efa	Pierce	Pyrs
Geoffrey	Sieffre	Ralph	Rawlff
George	Sior	Raymond	Raimwnt
Gerald	Gerallt	Reginald	Rheinallt
Griffith	Gruffudd	Richard	Rhisiart
Gwendoline	Gwendolen	Roderick	Rhodri
Guinevere	Gwenhwyfar	Roger	Rosser
Harold	Harallt	Rowland	Rolant
Hector	Echtor	Sibyl	Sibli
Helen	Elen	Thomas	Tomos
Henry	Harri	Tom	Twm
Howell	Hywel	Tristan	Trystan
Hugh	Huw	Victoria	Buddug
Humphrey	Wmffre	Walter	Gwallter
James	Iago	William	Gwilym
		Winifred	Gwenfrewi

COUNTRIES OF THE WORLD
GWLEDYDD Y BYD

America	Yr Amerig
Argentina	Arianin
Australia	Awstralia
Austria	Awstria
Belgium	Gwlad Belg
Britain	Prydain
Canaries	Ynysoedd Dedwydd
Egypt	Yr Aifft
England	Lloegr
France	Ffrainc
Germany	Yr Almaen
Greece	Gwlad Groeg
Holland	Isalmaen
Hungary	Hwngari
Iceland	Ynys yr Iâ
Ireland	Iwerddon
Italy	Yr Eidal
Jordan	Iorddonen
Lebanon	Libanus
Netherlands	Iseldiroedd
Norway	Norwy
New Zealand	Seland Newydd
Poland	Gwlad Pwyl
Russia	Rwsia
Scandinavia	Llychlyn
Scotland	Yr Alban
South Africa	De Affrig
Spain	Ysbaen
Switzerland	Swisdir
Turkey	Twrci
United States	Unol Daleithiau
Wales	Cymru

There are many other countries such as Canada, India, etc., where the name is the same in both English and Welsh.

SOME PLACE NAMES

Anglesey	Môn
Bath	Caerfaddon
Brecon	Aberhonddu
Bristol	Bryste
Caernarvon	Caernarfon
Cambridge	Caergrawnt
Canterbury	Caergaint
Cardiff	Caerdydd
Cardigan	Aberteifi
Carlisle	Caerliwelydd
Carmarthen	Caerfyrddin
Cheshire	Swydd Gaer
Chester	Caer
Chichester	Caerfuddai
Cirencester	Caer Geri
Clyde	Clud
Colchester	Caercolun
Cornwall	Cernyw
Coventry	Caerwenbir
Denbigh	Dinbych
Devon	Dyfnaint
Dover	Dofyr
Dublin	Dulyn
Dunbarton	Caer Aclud
Durham	Caerweir
Exeter	Caerwysg
Flint	Fflint
Glamorgan	Morgannwg
Glastonbury	Ynys Afallon
Gloucester	Caerloyw
Hereford	Henffordd
Ipswich	Caerorwel
Isle of Man	Manaw
Isle of Wight	Ynys Wyth
Kent	Caint
Lancaster	Caerhirfryn
Leicester	Caerlyr
Leominster	Llanllieni
Lichfield	Maesycyrff
Lincoln	Caerlwytgoed
Liverpool	Llynlleifiaid
Loch Lomond	Llyn Llumonwy
London	Llundain
Ludlow	Llwydlo
Manchester	Manceinion
Monmouth	Mynwy
Montgomery	Trefaldwyn
Oxford	Rhydychen
Pembroke	Penfro
Radnor	Maesyfed
Rochester	Caergraig
Salisbury	Caergaradog
Shrewsbury	Amwythig
Somerset	Gwlad yr Haf
Swansea	Abertawe
Winchester	Caerwynt
Worcester	Caerwrangon
York	Efrog

VOCABULARY

A

ble, to be *v*	gallu *v.n.*
bout *prp*	tua, ynglyn
bove	uwchben
bsent	absennol
bundant	helaeth
ccept v.	derbyn *v.n.*
ccident	damwain *f.*
ccidental	damweiniol
ccommodation	llety m.
cre	erw (-au) *f.*
cross	ar draws
ct	act (-au) *f.*
ct, to v.	actio
ddress	cyfeiriad (-au) *m.*
ddress, to	cyfeirio *v.n.*
dhere, to	glynu *v.n.*
dult	oedolyn (oedolion) *m.*
dvantage	mantais (manteision) *f.*
dventure	antur (-iaethau) *f.*
dvice	cyngor (cynghorion) *m.*
dvise, to	cynghori *v.n.*
eroplane	awyren (-nau) *f.*
fter	ar ôl; wedi
fternoon	pnawn (-iau) *m.*
	prynhawn (-iau)
fterwards	wedyn
gain	eto
gainst	yn erbyn
ge	oes (-au) *f.*
ge	oedran
gree, to	cytuno *v.n.*
id	cymorth
ir	aer, awyr *f.*
lder tree	gwernen *m.*
le	cwrw *m.*
ll	cyfan, cwbl, holl
long	ar hyd
lready	eisoes, yn barod
lso	hefyd
lways	bob amser
mongst	ymysg
mple	eang, digon
nd	a, ac, ag
ngel	angel (angylion) *m.*
nimal	anifail (anifeiliaid) *m.*
nnounce	cyhoeddi *v.n.*
nother	un arall
nswer	ateb (-ion) *m.*
nswer, to	ateb v.n.
nxiety	pryder (-on) *m.*
nything	rhywbeth
pple	afal (-au) *m.*
pple tree	pren afalau *m.*
pproach, to	nesu, agoshau *v.n.*
pricot	bricyllen (bricyll) *m.*
April	Ebrill

apron	ffedog (-au)
argue, to	dadlau *v.n.*
argument	dadl *f.*
arm	braich (breichiau) *f.*
armful	coflaid *f.*
arms	arfau *m.*
army	byddin (-oedd) *f.*
arrange, to	trefnu *v.n.*
arrive, to	cyrraedd *v.n.*
arrow	saeth (-au) *f.*
as	fel
ascend, to	dringo *v.n.*
ash	onnen (ynn) *m.*
ask, to	gofyn, holi *v.n.*
ass	asyn (-od) *m.*
assistance	help, cymorth
at	am, ger, ar
at all	o gwbl
attack, to	ymosod ar *v.n.*
attempt, to	ymgeisio *v.n.*
attempt	ymgais (ymgeision) *f.*
August	Awst
aunt	modryb *f.*
author	awdur (-on) *m.*
autumn	hydref
avoid, to	osgoi *v.n.*
awake	effro
awaken	deffro *v.n.*
away	i ffwrdd, ymaith
axe	bwyell (bwyeill) *f.*

B

baby	baban (-od) *m.*
back	cefn (-iau) *m.*
bacon	cig mochyn *m.*
bad drwg	
bag	bag (-iau) *m.*
bake, to	pobi *v.n.*
baker	pobydd *m.*
ball	pel (-i) *f.*
bandage	rhwymyn *m.*
bank	banc *m.*
bank (shore)	glan (-nau) *f.*
banner	baner (-i) *f.*
barber	barbwr *m.*
bargain	bargen (bargeinion)
bark, to	cyfarth *v.n.*
bark	cyfarthiad *m.*
basket	basged (-i) *f.*
bath	bath, baddon *m.*
bathe, to	ymdrochi *v.n.*
bathroom	ystafell molchi
bathing costume	dillad nofio
battery	batri *m.*
battle	brwydr (-au) *f.*
beach	traeth (-au)
beans	ffa

beard	barf (-au) *m.*
beat, to	curo *v.n.*
be, to	bod
beach	traeth
because	achos
bed	gwely (-au) *m.*
bedroom	ystafell wely *f.*
beech	hawydden (hawydd)
beef	cig eidion *m.*
beer	cwrw *m.*
before	o flaen
begin, to	dechrau *v.n.*
behave	ymddwyn *v.n.*
behaviour	ymddygiad
behind	tu ôl i
believe, to	credu *v.n.*
bell	cloch (clychau) *f.*
belong, to	perthyn *v.n.*
below	oddi tan
bench	mainc
bend	tro, troead (-au) *f.*
bend, to	plygu *v.n.*
beneath	islaw, dan
best	gorau
better	gwell
between	rhwng
bicycle	beic (-iau) *m.*
big	mawr
bill	cyfrif
birch	bedwen (bedw) *f.*
bird	aderyn (adar) *m.*
biscuit	bisged (-i) *f.*
bishop	esgob (-ion) *m.*
bite, to	cnoi *v.n.*
bitter	chwerw
black	du
blackberries	mwyar duon
blackboard	bwrdd du *(m)*
blackcurrants	cyrens duon
blacksmith	gôf (-aint) *m.*
blackthorn	draenen ddu
blanket	blanced (-i)
bless, to	bendithio *v.n.*
blessing	bendith (-ion) *f.*
blind	dall
blood	gwaed *m.*
blow, to	chwythu *v.n.*
blue	glas (gleision)
boat	cwch (cychod) *m.*
body	corff (cyrff) *m.*
boil, to	berwi *v.n.*
bone	asgwrn (esgyrn) *m.*
bonnet	bonet *m.*
book	llyfr (-au) *m.*
book, to	llogi *v.n.*
boot	esgid (-iau) *f.*
born, to be	geni *v.n.*
bosom	mynwes *f.*
bottle	potel (-i)
bottom	gwaelod *m.*

bowl	powlen (-ni) *f.*
box	bocs *m.*
box, to	paffio *v.n.*
boy	bachgen (bechgyn)
brain	ymenydd *m.*
brake	brêc (-iau) *m.*
branch	cangen (canghennau)
brave	dewr
bravery	dewrder *m.*
bread	bara *m.*
break, to	torri *v.n.*
breakfast	brecwast *m.*
breast	bron (-nau) *f.*
breath	anadl *m.*
breath, to	anadlu *v.n.*
breeze	awel (-on) *f.*
bride	priodferch *f.*
bridegroom	priodfab *m.*
bridge	pont (-ydd) *f.*
bridle	ffrwyn
bright	disglair, llachar, gloyw
bring, to	dod *v.n.*
brisket	barwyden
broadcast	darllediad (-au) *m.*
brook	nant (nentydd) *f.*
broom (flower)	banadl
broth	cawl *m.*
brother	brawd (brodyr) *m.*
brown	brown
brush	brwsh
bucket	bwced (-i) *m.*
build, to	adeiladu *v.n.*
building	adeilad (-au) *m.*
bull	tarw (teirw) *m.*
burden	baich (beichiau) *m.*
bus	bws *m.*
business	busnes *m.*
busy	prysur
but	ond
butcher	cigydd
butter	menyn *m.*
buy, to	prynu *v.n.*
by	wrth, erbyn

C

cabbage	bresych
cake	teisen, cacen (-ni) *f.*
calf	llo (-uau) *m.*
call, to	galw *v.n.*
calm	tawel
camera	camera (-u) *m.*
camp	gwersyll (-oedd) *m.*
camp, to	gwersylla *v.n.*
camper	gwersyllwr (gwersyll-wyr)
candle	canwyll (canhwyllau)
canvas	cynfas (-au) *m.*
capital (city)	prifddinas (-oedd)
capital (money)	cyfalaf
caravan	carafan (-nau)

ard	cerdyn (cardiau) m.
are	gofal (-on) m.
are, to	gofalu v.n.
areful	gofalus
areless	blêr, esgeulus
arpenter	saer (seiri) m.
arpet	carped (-i) m.
arriage	cerbyd (-au) m.
arry, to	cario v.n.
astle	castell (-i) m.
at	cath (-od) f.
athedral	eglwys gadeiriol f.
atch, to	dal v.n.
attle	gwartheg
auliflower	blodfresych
ave	ogof (-au) m.
elery	helogan
emetry	mynwent (-ydd) f.
entral	canolog
entre	canolfan (-au) m.
entury	canrif (-oedd) f.
aain	cadwyn (-i) f.
aair	cadair (cadeiriau) f.
aalk	sialc m.
aange, to	newid v.n.
aannel	sianel (-i) f.
aapel	capel (-i) m.
aapter	pennod (penodau) f.
aaracter	cymeriad (-au) m.
aarm	swyn m.
aat	sgwrs f.
aat, to	sgwrsio v.n.
aeap	rhâd
aeapest	rhataf
aeck, to	atal v.n.
aef	cogydd m.
aeek	boch (-au) f.
aeeky	digywilydd
aeese	caws m.
aeque	siec (-iau)
aeque book	llyfr sieciau
aerries	ceirios
aestnut	castanwydden
aicken	cyw iâr (cywion ieir) m.
aild	plentyn (plant) m.
ain	gên (-au) f.
aips	sglodion tatws
aocolate	siocled
aoice	dewis m.
aoir	côr (-au) m.
aoose, to	dewis v.n.
aurch	eglwys (-i) f.
nema	sinema (-u) m.
rcle	cylch
rcus	syrcas
ty	dinas (-oedd) f.
ass	dosbarth m.
ay	clai m.
ean	glân
ear	clir, eglur

cliff	clogwyn (-i)
climb, to	dringo v.n.
clock	cloc (-iau) m.
close, to	cau v.n.
closed	wedi cau
cloth	brethyn
clothes	dillad m. and f.
cloud	cwmwl (cymylau) m.
cloudy	cymylog
coal	glo m.
coast	arfordir m.
coat	côt (-iau) f.
cockerel	ceiliog (-od) m.
cocoa	coco
cod	cod, penfras
coffee	coffi
cold	oer, oerfel
cold (as 'flu)	annwyd m.
collar	coler (-i) m. and f.
collect, to	hel, casglu v.n.
colour	lliw (-iau)
colt	ebol (-ion) m.
column	colofn (-au) f.
comb	crib (-au) m. and f.
come, to	dod v.n.
comfortable	cyfforddus, cysurus
command, to	gorchymyn v.n.
committee	pwyllgor (-au) m.
company	cwmni (-au) m.
compare, to	cymharu v.n.
compel	gorfodi v.n.
compete, to	cystadlu v.n.
complain, to	cwyno v.n.
concert	cyngerdd m.
confuse, to	drysu v.n.
continue, to	parhau v.n.
control, to	rheoli v.n.
convenient	cyfleus, hwylus
cook, to	coginio v.n.
corn	]d m.
corner	cornel (-i), congl (-au)
correct	cywir
correct, to	cywiro v.n.
cottage	bwthyn (bythynnod) m.
cough, to	pesychu v.n.
cough	peswch m.
council	cyngor m.
count, to	rhifo, cyfrif v.n.
country	gwlad (gwledydd)
country	sir (-oedd) f.
course	cwrs (cyrsiau) m.
cover, to	cuddio v.n.
cover	clawr (cloriau) m.
cow	buwch (buchod) f.
cowshed	beudy (beudai) m.
crab	cranc
craft	crefft (-au) f.
cream	hufen
create, to	creu v.n.
cress	berw

cross	croes (-au) *f.*
cross, to	croesi *v.n.*
cruel	creulon
crumbs	briwsion
crowd	tyrfa (-oedd)
crown	coron (-au) *f.*
crown, to	coroni *v.n.*
cry, to	crio, llefain *v.n.*
cucumber	cucumer
cup	cwpan (-au) *f.*
cupboard	cwpwrdd *m.*
currants	cyrens
curtain	llen (-ni) *m.*
cushion	clustog (-au)
custard	cwstard
custom	arfer (-ion) *f.*
customer	cwsmer (-iaid) *m.*
cut, to	torri *v.n.*
cypress	cyprus

D

daily	dyddiol
dairy	llaethdy *m.*
dance	dawns (-iau) *f.*
dance, to	dawnsio *v.n.*
danger	perygl (-on) *m.*
dangerous	peryglus
dark	tywyll
date	dyddiad (-au) *m.*
dawn	gwawr, codiad yr haul
day	dydd (-iau) *m.*
deaf	byddar
dear	annwyl
death	angau, marwolaeth
debate	dadl (-euon) *f.*
debate, to	dadlau *v.n.*
deceit	twyll *m.*
deceive, to	twyllo *v.n.*
December	Rhagfyr
decide, to	penderfynu *v.n.*
deep	dwfn
deep freeze	rhewgell
defeat	gorchfygu *v.n.*
defect	diffyg (-ion) *m.*
degree	gradd (-au) *f.*
delicious	blasus
dentist	deintydd *m.*
deny, to	gwadu *v.n.*
deodorant	diaroglwr
depend, to	dibynnu *v.n.*
describe, to	disgrifio *v.n.*
description	disgrifiad (-au)
deserve, to	haeddu *v.n.*
desire	awydd, chwant *m.*
desire, to	dymuno, chwennych *v.n.*
desk	desg (-iau) *f.*
dessert	pwdin
dessertspoon	llwy bwdin
destroy, to	difetha, chwalu *v.n.*

die, to	marw *v.n.*
difference	gwahaniaeth (-au) *m.*
different	gwahanol
difficult	anodd
dig, to	cloddio, tyllu, palu *v.n.*
dinner	cinio
dine, to	ciniawa *v.n.*
direction	cyfeiriad (-au) *m.*
dirt	baw
dirty	budr, brwnt
disappear	diflannu *v.n.*
dish	llestr, llestri *m.*
disinfectant	diheintiwr
district	ardal (-oedd) *f.*
ditch	ffos(-ydd) *f.*
do, to	gwneud *v.n.*
doctor	meddyg (-on) *m.*
dog	ci (c[n) *m.*
doll	doli *f.*
donkey	asyn (-od)
door	drws (drysau) *m.*
double	dwbwl
doubt	amheuaeth
doubt, to	amau *v.n.*
doubtful	amheus
doubtless	diamau
down	i lawr
drag, to	llusgo *v.n.*
dragon	draig
drama	drama (-u) *f.*
draper's shop	siop ddillad
draw, to	darlunio *v.n.*
drawer	drôr *m.*
dress, to	gwisgo *v.n.*
dress	gwisg (-oedd) *f.*
drink, to	yfed *v.n.*
drink	diod (-ydd) *f.*
drive, to	gyrru *v.n.*
drop	diferyn (diferion) *m.*
drop, to	disgyn *v.n.*
drown, to	boddi *v.n.*
dry	sych
dry, to	sychu *v.n.*
duck	hwyaden (hwyaid) *f.*
dumb	mud
dust	llwch *m.*
dynamo	deinamo

E

ear	clust (-iau) *m.* and *f.*
early	cynnar
earth (world)	daear *f.*
earth (soil)	pridd
east	dwyrain
easy	hawdd, rhwydd
eat, to	bwyta *v.n.*
ebb	trai *m.*
echo	adlef *f.* adlais *m.*
education	addysg *f.*
educate, to	addysgu *v.n.*

fort	ymdrech (-ion) f.	fall, to	disgyn v.n.
g	wy (-au) m.	family	teulu (-oedd) m.
ght	wyth	famine	newyn m.
ghteen	un deg wyth	fan	ffan
der tree	ysgawen (ysgaw)	fan belt	belt y ffan
ectric	trydan	far	pell
ectricity	trydan m.	farm	ffarm (ffermydd) f.
even	un deg un	farmer	ffermwr m.
m	llwyfen	farmhouse	ffermdy m.
npty	gwag	fast	cyflym, sydyn
npty, to	gwagio v.n.	fat	tew
d	diwedd m.	father	tad (-au) m.
d, to	gorffen, diweddu v.n.	fault	bai (beiau) m.
ding	diweddglo m.	fear	ofn (-au) m.
emy	gelyn (-ion) m.	fear, to	ofni v.n.
nglish	Season	feast	gwledd (-oedd) f.
nglish (language)	Saesneg	feather	pluen (plu) f.
nglishman	Sais	February	Chwefror
nglishwoman	Saesnes	feel, to	teimlo v.n.
gine	injan	female	benyw (-od) f.
njoy, to	mwynhau v.n.	fetch, to	nôl, estyn v.n.
ough	digon	few	ychydig
rol, to	ymaelodi v.n.	field	cae (-au) m.
nvelope	amlen (-ni) f.	fifteen	un deg pump
ror	gwall m.	fifty	pum deg
scape, to	dianc v.n.	fight, to	ymladd, cwffio v.n.
pecially	enwedig	fill, to	llenwi v.n.
tablish, to	sefydlu v.n.	film	ffilm
tablishment	sefydliad (-au)	fine	braf
ening	noson (nosweithiau)	finger	bys (-edd) m.
ent	digwyddiad (-au) m.	finger nail	ewin (-edd) m.
er	byth, erioed	finish, to	gorffen v.n.
ery	pob, bob	fire	tân (-au) m.
erybody	pawb	firm	cadarn
erything	popeth m.	fish	pysgodyn (pysgod) m.
ve	dafad (defaid) f.	flag	baner (-i) f.
xact	manwl	flame	fflam (-au) f.
xactly	hollol	flat	gwastad
xamination	arholiad (-au) m.	flesh	cnawd m.
xcellent	ardderchog, rhagorol	flood	llif (-ogydd) m.
xcess	gormod m.	floor	llawr (lloriau) m.
xcuse	esgus (-ion)	flour	blawd (-iau) m.
xcuse, to	esgusodi v.n.	flow, to	llifo v.n.
xercise, to	ymarfer v.n.	flower	blodyn (blodau) m.
xpect, to	disgwyl v.n.	flower, to	blodeuo v.n.
xpensive	drud	fly	pryf (-aid)
xperience	profiad (-au) m.	fly, to	ehedeg, hedfan v.n.
xtinguish, to	diffodd v.n.	foam	ewyn
ye	llygad (llygaid) m.	folk	gwerin (-oedd) f.
		follow, to	dilyn v.n.
		fond	hoff
ce	wyneb (-au) m.	food	bwyd
cilities	cyfleusterau	fool	ffwl
ctory	ffatri (-oedd)	foolish	gwirion
il, to	methu v.n.	foot	troed (traed) f.
ir	teg	foot (measure)	troedfedd (-i) m.
irly	gweddol	for	i
iry	tylwyth teg	force	grym m.
ith	ffydd f.	forecast	rhagolygon
ithful	ffyddlon	forehead	talcen (-i)

foreigner	estron (-iaid) *m.*
forest	coedwig (-oedd)
forget, to	anghofio *v.n.*
forgive, to	maddau *v.n.*
fork	fforc *f.*
form	ffurflen (-ni)
form, to	ffurfio *v.n.*
formerly	gynt
fort	caer (-au) *f.*
fortnight	pythefnos
fortunate	lwcus, ffodus
foundation	sylfaen, sail
four	pedwar
fourteen	un deg pedwar
fox	llwynog (-od) *m.*
freeze, to	rhewi *v.n.*
fresh	ffres
Friday	dydd Gwener
fridge	oergell (-i) *f.*
friend	ffrind (-iau) *m.*
frock	ffrog (-iau) *f.*
from	o
from the	o'r
front	ffrynt *m.*
frost	barug
fruit	ffrwyth (-au) *m.*
fruitful	ffrwythlon
fruit juice	sudd ffrwythau
fry, to	ffrio *v.n.*
frying pan	padell ffrio
full	llawn
funny	doniol
fur	blewyn (blew) *m.*
furniture	dodrefn *m.*

G

gain, to	ennill *v.n.*
gains	enillion *m.*
gallon	galwyn (-i) *m.*
gallop, to	carlamu *v.n.*
game	gˆm (-au) *f.*
gap	bwlch (bylchau) *m.*
garage	garej *f.*
garden	gardd (gerddi) *f.*
garden, to	garddio *v.n.*
garlic	garlleg
gas	nwy
gate	gât, giât, clwyd, adwy
generation	cenhedlaeth *f.*
gentle	addfwyn
gentleman	g[r bonheddig *m.*
get, to	cael *v.n.*
gift	anrheg (-ion) *f.*
ginger	sinsir
girl	merch (-ed) *f.*
give, to	rhoi *v.n.*
glad	balch, llon
glass	gwydr (-au) *m.*
glory	gogoniant *m.*
glove	maneg (menig)

go, to	mynd *v.n.*
goat	gafr (geifr) *f.*
God	Duw
good	da
goodness	daioni *m.*
goods	nwyddau
goose	gwydd (-au) *f.*
gooseberries	eirin Mair (gwsberis)
gorse	eithin
government	llywodraeth (-au) *f.*
gradual	graddol
grand-daughter	[yres *f.*
grandfather	taid *m.*
grandmother	nain *f.*
grandson	[yr *m.*
grapes	grawnwin
grapefruit	grawnffrwyth
grasp, to	gafael, cydio *v.n.*
grave	bedd (-au) *m.*
gravy	grefi
grave, to	pori *v.n.*
greedy	gwancus, barus
green	gwyrdd
grey	llwyd
grocer	groser
ground	daear, tir
group	gr[p
grove	llwyn (-i) *m.*
grow, to	tyfu v.n.
guide	arweinydd (-ion) *m.*

H

haddock	hadog
hair	gwallt *m.*
hake	cegddu
half	hanner *m.*
hall	neuadd (-au) *f.*
ham	ham
hammer	morthwyl (-ion) *m.*
hand	llaw (dwylo) *f.*
handicrafts	gwaith llaw *m.*
handkerchief	hances (-i) *f.*
handsome	golygus
hang, to	hongian, crogi *v.n.*
happen, to	digwydd *v.n.*
harbour	harbwr
hard	caled
harm	niwed *m.*
harp	telyn (-au) *f.*
harvest	cynhaeaf (-au) *m.*
hat	het (-iau) *f.*
have, to	cael *v.n.*
hawthorn	draenen wen
hay	gwair *m.*
hazel	collen (cyll)
head	pen (-nau) *m.*
headache	cur pen *m.*
health	iechyd *m.*
healthy	iach
hear, to	clywed *v.n.*

:art	calon (-nau) *f.*	ill	sâl, tost, gwael
:arth	aelwyd (ydd) *f.*	important	pwysig
:at	gwrês *m.*	impression	argraff (-iadau) *f.*
:at, to	poethi *v.n.*	in	yn, mewn
:ather	grug	inch	modfedd (-i)
:aven	nefoedd *f.*	include, to	cynnwys *v.n.*
:avy	trwm	independence	annibyniaeth
:dge	gwrych (-oedd) *m.*	independent	annibynnol
:ight	uchder, taldra	industrial	diwydiannol
:ll	uffern	industrious	dyfal
:lp	cymorth	industry	diwydiant (diwydiannau) *m.*
:lp, to	cynorthwyo *v.n.*		
:n	iâr (ieir) *f.*	inexperienced	dibrofiad
:rbs	perlysiau	inhabitant	trigolyn (trigolion)
:re	yma	inhospitable	digroeso
:rrings	penwaig	ink	inc
.de, to	cuddio *v.n.*	inn	tafarn (-au) *m.* and *f.*
.gh	uchel	inquire, to	holi *v.n.*
.ghest	uchaf	inspector	arolygwr (arolygwyr) *m.*
.ll	rhiw (-iau); bryn (-iau)	in spite of	er gwaethaf
.ndrance	rhwystr (-au) *m.*	instrument	offeryn (-nau) *m.*
.re, to	llogi *v.n.*	intend, to	bwriadu *v.n.*
.storical	hanesyddol	intention	bwriad (-au) *m.*
.story	hanes	interest	diddordeb
ob	pentan (-au) *m.*	interest, to	diddori *v.n.*
old, to	gafael v.n.	interesting	diddorol
ole	twll (tyllau) *m.*	international	rhyngwladol
olidays	gwyliau *f.*	invitation	gwahoddiad (-au)
ollow	pant (-iau) *m.*	invite, to	gwahodd *v.n.*
ome	cartref (-i) *m.*	iron	haearn
omewards	adref	iron, to	smwddio *v.n.*
oney	mêl *m.*	is	mae
ook	bachyn (bachau)	island	ynys (-oedd) *f.*
ope	gobaith (gobeithion) *m.*		
ope, to	gobeithio *v.n.*	**J**	
orizon	gorwel (-ion) *m.*	jam	jam
orn	corn (cyrn) *m.*	January	Ionawr
orse	ceffyl (-au) *m.*	job	gwaith (gweithiau)
orseshoe	pedol (-au) *f.*	join, to	cysylltu, ymaelodi, uno *v.n.*
ospitable	croesawus		
ospital	ysbyty (ysbytai) *m.*	joint	cyswllt, cymal *m.*
ot	poeth	jolly	llawen
otel	gwesty (gwestai) *m.*	journey	taith (teithiau) *f.*
our	awr (oriau) *f.*	journey, to	teithio *v.n.*
ouse	t] (tai) *m.*	joy	llawenydd *m.*
ousework	gwaith t]	joyful	llawen
ow	sut	judge	barnwr (barnwyr) *m.*
undred	cant (cannoedd) *m.*	judge, to	barnu *v.n.*
unt, to	hela *v.n.*	judgement	barn *f.*
urry	brys *m.*	jug	jwg, piser
urry, to	brysio *v.n.*	juice	sudd
usband	g[r (g[yr) *m.*	July	Gorffennaf
ymn	emyn (-au) *m.*	jump, to	neidio *v.n.*
		June	Mehefin
e	iâ, rhew *m.*	**K**	
e cream	hufen iâ	keep, to	cadw *v.n.*
y	rhewi	kettle	tegell (-i) *m.*
ea	syniad (-au) *m.*	key	allwedd, goriad (-au) *f.*
	os	kick	cic

41

kick, to	cicio *v.n.*
kidney	aren (-nau)
kill, to	lladd *v.n.*
kind	caredig
kind (sort)	math (-au) *m.*
kindness	caredigrwydd
king	brenin (brenhinoedd) *m.*
kinsfolk	tylwyth (-au) *m.*
kiss	cusan (-au) *f.*
kiss, to	cusanu *v.n.*
kitchen	cegin (-au) *m.* and *f.*
knee	pen-glin (-au) *m.*
knife	cyllell (cyllyll) *f.*
knight	marchog (-ion) *m.*
knock, to	cnocio *v.n.*
knot	cwlwm (clymau) *m.*
know, to	gwybod, adnabod *v.n.*
knowledge	gwybodaeth *f.*

L

labour	llafur *m.*
lad	llanc (-iau) *m.*
lake	llyn (-noedd) *m.*
lamb	oen ([yn) *m.*
lame	clôff
land	tir (-oedd) *m.*
land, to	glanio *v.n.*
language	iaith (ieithoedd) *f.*
large	mawr
last	olaf
last night	neithiwr
last year	llynedd
late	hwyr, diweddar
laugh, to	chwerthin *v.n.*
laughter	chwerthin *m.*
laurel	llawryf
lavatory	t] bach
law, a	deddf (-ai) *f.*
law, the	y gyfraith *f.*
lawn	lawnt (-iau) *f.*
lay, to (eggs)	dodwy *v.n.*
lazy	diog
leaf	deilen (dail) *f.*
leak, to	gollwng *v.n.*
learn, to	dysgu *v.n.*
leave, to	gadael *v.n.*
leek	cenhinen (cennin)
left	chwith
leg	coes (-au) *f.*
leisure	hamdden *m.*
lemon	lemon
lemonade	lemonêd
length	h]d *m.*
lesson	gwers (-i) *f.*
letter	llythyr (-au) *m.*
lettuce	letysen (letys)
level	gwastad
library	llyfrgell (-oedd) *f.*
licence	trwydded (-i)
lie	celwydd (-au) *m.*

lie, to	dweud celwydd
lie, to (down)	gorwedd *v.n.*
lift	esgynfa
lift, to	codi *v.n.*
light, to	cynnau, goleuo *v.n.*
light	golau
light (weight)	ysgafn
lightning	mellten (mellt) *f.*
like	fel, tebyg
like, to	hoffi *v.n.*
line	llinell (-au) *f.*
lion	llew (-od) *m.*
lip	gwefus (-au) *f.*
list	rhestr (-au) *f.*
listen to	gwrando *v.n.*
literature	llên
little, a	ychydig
little (small)	bychan, bach
live, to	byw *v.n.*
liver	iau, afu
loaf	torth *f.*
loan	benthyciad (-au) *m.*
loan, to	benthyg *v.n.*
lobster	cimwch (cimychiaid)
local	lleol
lock	clo (-eau) *m.*
lock, to	cloi *v.n.*
lonely	unig
long	hir
longing	hiraeth
look, to	edrych *v.n.*
look for, to	chwilio *v.n.*
lord	arglwydd (-i) *m.*
lorry	lori
lose, to	colli *v.n.*
lost	ar goll
lounge	lolfa *f.*
love	cariad *m.*
love, to	caru *v.n.*
lovely	hyfryd
lovespoon	llwy garu
low	isel
low, to	brefu *v.n.*
lower	îs
lower, to	gostwng *v.n.*
luck	lwc

M

machine	peiriant (peiriannau) *m*
mackerel	macrell (mecryll)
magazine	cylchgrawn
maid	morwyn (-ion) *f.*
make, to	gwneud *v.n.*
male voice choir	côr meibion
man	dyn (-ion) *m.*
manner	ymddygiad
manner (form)	dull (-iau) *m.*
many	llawer
map	map (-iau) *m.*
March	Mawrth

march	gorymdaith	mouse	llygoden (llygod) *f.*
march, to	ymdeithio *v.n.*	mouth	ceg (-au) *f.*
mare	caseg (cesyg) *f.*	move, to	symud *v.n.*
market	marchnad (-oedd) *f.*	much	cymaint
marmalade	marmaled	mud	mwd
marry, to	priodi *v.n.*	mulberry	merwydden
marriage	priodas (-au) *f.*	mushrooms	madarch
masculine	gwrywaidd	music	cerddoriaeth
master	meistr (-i) *m.*	musician	cerddor (-ion) *m.*
mat	mat (-iau)	must	rhaid
material	defnydd (-iau) *m.*	mustard	mwstard
matter	mater, peth, achos	mutton	cig dafad
May	Mai		
me	mi, fi	**N**	
meal	pryd o fwyd *m.*	naked	noeth
mean, to	golygu *v.n.*	name	enw (-au) *m.*
meaning	ystyr (-on) *m.* and *f.*	name, to	enwi v.n.
measles	frech goch	narrow	cul
measure	mesur (-au) *m.*	nasty	câs
measure, to	mesur *v.n.*	nation	cenedl (cenhedloedd) *f.*
meat	cig (-oedd) *m.*	national	cenedlaethol
mechanic	peiriannydd *m.*	natural	naturiol
medicine	ffisig, moddion *m.*	nature	natur *f.*
meet, to	cyfarfod, cwrdd *v.n.*	naughty	drwg
meeting	cyfarfod (-ydd) *m.*	near	agos
melody	alaw (-on) *f.*	near, to draw	agoshau *v.n.*
melon	melwn	nearer	nes, agosach
melt, to	toddi *v.n.*	nearest	agosaf
member	aelod (-au) *m.*	nearly	bron
memory	côf (-ion) *m.*	need, to	eisiau *v.n.*
menu	bwydlen *f.*	needle	nodwydd (-au) *f.*
merry	llon, hwyliog	neigh, to	gwehyru *v.n.*
message	neges (-au) *f.*	neighbour	cymydog (cymdogion) *m.*
midday	hanner dydd *m.*	neither	chwaith
middle	canol *m.*	nest	nyth (-od)
midnight	hanner nos *m.*	net	rhwyd (-au)
mile	milltir (-oedd)	new	newydd *m.*
milk	llefrith, llaeth *m.*	news	newyddion *m.*
milk, to	godro *v.n.*	newspaper	papur newydd
milkman	dyn llefrith	next	nesaf
mill	melin (-au) *f.*	nice	neis
minister	gweinidog (-ion) *m.*	night	nos (-weithiau) *f.*
minute	munud (-au) *m.* and *f.*	nine	naw
mirror	drych (-au) *m.*	nineteen	un deg naw
mist	niwl (-oedd) *m.*	noise	s[n
mistake	camgymeriad (-au)	north	gogledd *m.*
misty	niwlog	nose	trwyn (-au) *m.*
mix, to	cymysgu *v.n.*	nostril	ffroen (-au) *f.*
mixture	cymysgedd	note	nodyn (nodiadau)
moist	tamp, llaith	notes (music)	nodau
Monday	dydd Llun	nothing	dim
money	arian, prês *m.*	notice	sylw, rhybudd
month	mis (-oedd) *m.*	notice, to	sylwi v.n.
noon	lleuad (-au) *f.*	now	rwan, nawr
more	rhagor, chwaneg, mwy	novel	nofel (-au) *f.*
morning	bore (-au) *m.*	November	Tachwedd
most	mwyaf	nurse	nyrs (-iau) *f.*
mostly	gan mwyaf	nurse, to	magu *v.n.*
mountain	mynydd (-oedd) *m.*	nut	cneuen (cnau) *f.*

O

oak	derwen (derw) *f.*
oats	ceirch
obedience	ufudd-dod
obedient	ufudd
obey, to	ufuddhau *v.n.*
observation	sylw (-adau)
observe, to	sylwi *v.n.*
occasional	ambell
October	Hydref
off	i ffwrdd
offence	trosedd (-au) *m.*
offend, to	troseddu *v.n.*
offended, to be	digio *v.n.*
office	swyddfa (swyddfeydd) *f.*
officer *m.*	swyddog (-ion) *m.*
often	aml
oil	olew, oel *m.*
ointment	eli
old	hen
old, to grow	heneiddio *v.n.*
on	ar
once	unwaith
once	un
onions	nionod, winwns
only	dim ond, unig
onward	ymlaen
open	agored
open, to	agor *v.n.*
opportunity	cyfle *m.*
or	neu
orange	oren (-nau) *m.* and *f.*
orange juice	sudd oren
orchard	perllan (-nau) *f.*
orchestra	cerddorfa *f.*
order	trefn, gorchymyn
order, to	gorchymyn *v.n.*
ordinary	cyffredin
other	arall, llall
ounce	owns
out	allan
our	ein
oven	ffwrn (-esi)
over	dros
over heat, to	poethi *v.n.*
owner	perchennog (perchen-ogion) *u.*
own, to	meddu, perchnogi *v.n.*

P

page	tudalen (-nau) *m.*
paint	paent *m.*
pain	poen (-au) *m.* and *f.*
pair	pâr (parau) *m.*
palace	plas (-au) *m.*
palm tree	palmwydden *f.*
pan	padell (-i)
paper	papur (-au) *m.*
parcel	parsel (-i) *m.*

parish	plwyf (-i) *m.*
park	parc (-iau) *m.*
park, to	parcio *v.n.*
parliament	senedd *f.*
parsnip	pannas
part	rhan (-nau) *f.*
party (faction)	plaid (pleidiau) *f.*
party (social)	parti (-on) *f.*
pass	bwlch
pass, to	pasio *v.n.*
pasture	porfa (porfeydd) *f.*
pasty	tarten
path	llwybr (-au) *m.*
patience	amynedd
patient	amyneddgar
pavement	palmant (palmentyd(
pavilion	pafiliwn *m.*
pay, to	talu *v.n.*
payment	taliad (-au) *m.*
peace	heddwch *m.*
peaches	eirin gwlanog
peak	pîg
pears	gellyg
pear tree	pren gellygen *f.*
peas	p]s
pencil	pensil *m.*
penny	ceiniog (-au) *f.*
people	pobl (-oedd) *m.*
pepper	pupur
perfect	perffaith
perfection	perffeithrwydd
perfume	perarogl
perhaps	efallai, hwyrach
period	adeg (-au) *f.*
permission	caniatâd
permit, to	caniatau *v.n.*
person	person
perspiration	chw]s *m.*
perspire, to	chwysu *v.n.*
petrol	petrol
pheasant	ceiliog y coed *m.*
photograph	llun (-iau)
picture	darlun (-iau) *m.*
pie	tarten
piece	darn (-au) *m.*
pig	mochyn (moch) *m.*
pillow	clustog (-au) *m.*
pills	tabledi
pin	pin (-nau) *m.*
pine	pinwydd (pîn) *f.*
pineapple	pîn afal *f.*
pint	peint (-iau) *m.*
pit	pwll (pyllau) *m.*
pity	trueni *m.*
pity, to	tosturio, gresynu *v.n.*
place	lle (-oedd) *m.*
plaice	lleden
plan	cynllun (-iau) *m.*
plant, to	plannu *v.n.*

parents	rhieni	plaster	plastr
plate	plât (-iau) *m.*	promise, to	addo *v.n.*
play	chwarae (-on)	proof	prawf (profion) *m.*
play, to	chwarae *v.n.*	proposition	cynigiad (cynigion) *m.*
player	chwaraewr *m.*	prose	rhyddiaeth *f.*
playtime	amser chwarae	proud	balch
pleasant	dymunol	prove, to	profi *v.n.*
please	os gwelwch yn dda	public, the	cyhoedd
please, to	plesio *v.n.*	public	cyhoeddus
pleasure	pleser (-au) *m.*	public conven-	
plough	aradr (erydr) *f.*	ience	cyfleusterau cyhoeddus
plug	plwg (-iau) *m.*	public footpath	llwybr cyhoeddus
plum	eiran (eirin)	pudding	pwdin
poach, to	potsho *v.n.*	pull, to	tynnu *v.n.*
pocket	poced (-i) *f.*	pump	pwmp
poet	bardd (beirdd) *m.*	punctual	prydlon
point	blaen (-au) *m.*	punish, to	cosbi *v.n.*
point, to	pwyntio *v.n.*	punishment	cosb (-au) *f.*
police	heddlu	pupil	disgybl (-ion) *n.*
policeman	plisman	pure	pur
pony trekking	merlota	purpose	diben (-ion) *m.*
poor	tlawd		amcan (amcanion)
poorly (ill)	gwael	put, to	rhoi, dodi *v.n.*
poplar	poplysen *f.*		
popular	poblogaidd	**Q**	
population	poblogaeth *f.*	quarrel	ffrae (-on) *f.*
pork	porc *m.*	quarrel, to	ffraeo *v.n.*
porridge	uwd	quarry (slate)	chwarel (-i) *f.*
post	postyn, stanc	quarry (victim)	ysglyfaeth *m.*
post, to	postio *v.n.*	quart	chwart
postal order	order post	quarter	chwarter (-i) *m.*
post office	swyddfa bost	quay	cei
potato	tysen (tatws) *f.*	queen	brenhines (-au) *f.*
potter	crochennydd *m.*	question	cwestiwn (cwestiynnau)
pottery	crochenwaith		*m.*
pound	pwys (-i) *m.*	quick	sydyn
pound (sterling)	punt (punnoedd) *f.*	quickly	sydyn
pour, to	tywallt *v.n.*	quiet	tawel, llonydd
poverty	tlodi	quietly	tawel, llonydd
power	gallu (-oedd), nerth *m.*	quietness	tawelwch, llonyddwch
practice	practis *m.*		
practise, to	ymarfer *v.n.*	**R**	
prawns	corgimwch	race	tras
pray, to	gweddio *v.n.*	race, to	rasio *v.n.*
preach, to	pregethu *v.n.*	radio	radio, diwyfr *m.*
preacher	pregethwr *m.*	railway	rheilffordd (rheil-
prepare, to	paratoi *v.n.*		ffyrdd) *m.*
prescription	cyfarwyddyd	rain	glaw (-ogydd) *m.*
present	anrheg	rain, to	glawio, bwrw glaw *m.*
press, to	gwasgu *v.n.*	raincoat	côt law
pretty	tlws, pert	ram	hwrdd (hyrddod) *m.*
price	prîs (-iau) *m.*	raspberries	mafon
primary school	ysgol gynradd	rates	trethi
print, to	argraffu *v.n.*	rather	braidd
prison	carchar	reach, to	cyrraedd, estyn *v.n.*
prisoner	carcharor (-ion) *m.*	read, to	darllen *v.n.*
prize	gwobr (-au) *f.*	reader	darllenydd m.
produce, to	cynhyrchu *v.n.*	ready	parod
product	cynnyrch (cynhyrchion)	reap, to	medi *v.n.*
programme	rhaglen (-ni) *f.*	reason	rheswm (rhesymau) *m.*

promise	addewid (-ion) *f.*
receive, to	derbyn *v.n.*
recitation	adroddiad
recite, to	adrodd *v.n.*
recognize, to	adnabod *v.n.*
recommend, to	cynghori, argymell *v.n.*
red	coch
red currants	cyrens coch
reduce, to	lleihau *v.n.*
region	bro (-ydd) *f.*
register	cofrestr
register, to	cofrestru
rejoice, to	gorfoleddu *v.n.*
religion	crefydd (-au) *f.*
remarkable	hynod
remember, to	cofio *v.n.*
repair, to	trwsio *v.n.*
repent, to	edifarhau *v.n.*
report	adroddiad (-au)
report, to	gohebu, adrodd *v.n.*
reserve, to	llogi *v.n.*
respect	parch
respect, to	parchu *v.n.*
rest	gorffwys
rest, to	gorffwyso *v.n.*
restaurant	ystafell fwyta
return, to	dychwelyd, dod nôl *v.n.*
reverend	parchedig
rice	reis
rich	cyfoethog
ride, to	marchogaeth
right (side)	de
right (correct)	cywir, iawn
right (demand)	hawl (-iau) *f.*
ring	modrwy (-au) *f.*
ring, to	canu *v.n.*
ripe	aeddfed
rise, raise, to	codi *v.n.*
river	afon (-ydd) *f.*
road	ffordd, lôn, heol
roast, to	rhostio *v.n.*
rock	craig (creigiau) *f.*
rod	gwialen
romance	rhamant (-au) *f.*
roof	to (-iau) m.
room	ystafell (-oedd) *f.*
rope	rhaff (-au) *f.*
rose	rhosyn (-nau) *m.*
round	crwn
row	rhes (-i) *f.*
rowan tree	pren criafol
rule	rheol (-au) *f.*
rule, to	rheoli *v.n.*
rumour	sôn, sî *m.*
run, to	rhedeg *v.n.*
rush, to	rhuthro *v.n.*

S

sack	sach (-au)
sad	digalon, trist

reason, to	rhesymu *v.n.*
safe	diogel
safety	diogelwch
sail	hwyl (-iau) *f.*
sail, to	hwylio *v.n.*
saint	sant (saint) *m.*
sale	arwerthiant
salmon	eog
salt	halen *m.*
salty	hallt
sand	tywod *m.*
sandy	tywodlyd
sandwich	brechdan (-au)
satisfy, to	bodloni *v.n.*
Saturday	dydd Sadwrn
sauce	saws
saucer	soser (-i) *f.*
sausage	selsyg
save, to	achub *v.n.*
say, to	dweud *v.n.*
saying	dywediad (-au)
scarcity	prinder
school	ysgol (-ion) *m.*
scissors	siswrn (sisyrnau) *m.*
sea	môr (-oedd)
seagull	gwylan (-od) *f.*
seal	morlo (-i) *m.*
search, to	chwilio *v.n.*
seaside	glan y môr
season	tymor (tymhorau) *m.*
seat	sedd (-au) *f.*
second (2nd)	ail
second (time)	eiliad (-au) *m.* and *f.*
secretary	ysgrifennydd (ysgrif-enyddion) *m.*
see, to	gweld *v.n.*
seed	had (-au) *m.*
seek, to	ceisio *v.n.*
sell, to	gwerthu *v.n.*
send, to	anfon, gyrru *v.n.*
sense	synnwyr (synhwyrau) *m.*
sentence	brawddeg (-au) *f.*
September	Medi
serious	difrifol
sermon	pregeth (-au) *f.*
settle, to	setlo *v.n.*
seven	saith
seventeen	un deg saith
severe	llym
sew, to	gwnio *v.n.*
sex	rhyw
shade, shadow	cysgod (-ion) *m.*
shake, to	ysgwyd *v.n.*
shampoo	sebon gwallt
shape	siap, llun
shapeless	di-lun
share, to	rhannu *v.n.*
sharp	miniog
sheep	dafad (defaid) *f.*
sheepfold	corlan (-nau) *f.*

saddle	cyfrwy	shelf	silff (-oedd) *f.*
shell	crogan (cregyn)	so	felly
shepherd	bugail (bugeiliaid) *m.*	soap	sebon (-au) *f.*
shine, to	disgleirio	soap, to	seboni *v.n.*
shine, to (sun)	tywynnu *v.n.*	society	cymdeithas (-au) *f.*
ship	llong (-au) *f.*	soft	meddal
shirt	crys (-au) *m.*	soften, to	meddalu *v.n.*
shoe	esgid (-iau)	soil	pridd *m.*
shoe, to	pedoli *v.n.*	sole	lleden *m.*
shoot, to	saethu *v.n.*	someone	rhywun *m.*
shop	siop (-au) *f.*	something	rhywbeth *m.*
shop, to	siopa *v.n.*	sometime	rhywbryd *m.*
shore	traeth (-au)	sometimes	weithiau *m.*
short	byr	somewhere	rhywle *m.*
shoulder	ysgwydd (-au) *m.*	son	mab, meibion *m.*
shout, to	gweiddi *v.n.*	song	can (euon) *f.*
show	sioe (-au) *f.*	sort	mâth (-au) *m.*
show, to	dangos *v.n.*	sort out, to	dosbarthu *v.n.*
shower	cawod (-ydd) *f.*	soul	enaid (eneidiau) *f.*
shrimps	berdysa	sound	s[n *m.*
shut, to	cau *v.n.*	soup	cawl *m.*
side	ochr (-au) *f.*	sour	sur
sight	golwg *f.*	sow	hwch (hychod) *f.*
sign, to	arwyddo *v.n.*	sow, to	hau *v.n.*
sign	arwydd (-ion)	spade	rhaw (-iau) *f.*
silence	distawrwydd *m.*	sparing	cynnil
silk	sidan (-au) *m.*	speak, to	siarad *v.n.*
silver	arian	spend, to (money)	gwario *v.n.*
silver birch	bedw arian	spend, to (time)	treulio *v.n.*
similar	tebyg	spirit	ysbryd (-ion) *m.*
sin	pechod (-au) *m.*	spoon	llwy (au) *f.*
sin, to	pechu *v.n.*	Spring	Gwanwyn *m.*
sinew	gewyn (-nau) *m.*	square	sgwâr
sing, to	canu *v.n.*	stage	llwyfan (-nau) *f.*
single	unigol	stand, to	sefyll *v.n.*
sink, to	suddo *v.n.*	star	seren (sêr) *f.*
sister	chwaer (chwiorydd) *f.*	start, to	cychwyn *v.n.*
sit, to	eistedd *v.n.*	station	gorsaf (-oedd) *f.*
site	maes (meusydd)	stay, to	aros *v.n.*
six	chwech	steak	golwyth
sixteen	un deg chwech	steel	dur *m.*
size	maint	step	cam (-au) *m.*
skin	croen (crwyn) *m.*	step (stairs)	gris (-iau) *m.*
skirt	sgert (-i)	step, to	camu *v.n.*
sky	awyr	still	llonydd
sleep	cwsg	stillness	llonyddwch *m.*
sleep, to	cysgu *v.n.*	stocking	hosan (-nau) *m.*
slow	araf	stone	carreg (cerrig) *f.*
small	bach, bychan	stony	caregog
smaller	llai	stool	stôl (-ion)
smallpox	frech wen	stop, to	stopio, aros *v.n.*
smile	gwên (gwenau) *f.*	stop!	arhoswch!
smile, to	gwenu *v.n.*	storm	storm (-ydd) *f.*
smoke	m[g	story	stori (-au) *f.*
smoke, to	ysmygu, smocio *v.n.*	straight	syth, union
smooth	llyfn	strange	rhyfedd
snake	neidr (nadroedd) *f.*	straw	gwellt
snow	eira *m.*	strawberries	mefus
snow, to	bwrw eira *v.n.*	street	stryd (-oedd) *f.*
Snowdon	Yr Wyddfa	strike, to	taro *v.n.*

47

Snowdonia	Eryri
strong	cryf
studio	stiwdio *f.*
study, to	astudio *v.n.*
subject	pwnc (pynciau) *m.*
succeed, to	llwyddo *v.n.*
sudden	sydyn
suffer, to	dioddef *v.n.*
sugar	siwgwr *m.*
sum	swm (symiau) *m.*
summer	haf (-au)
summit	copa
sun	haul *m.*
Sunday	dydd Sul
sunny	heulog
supper	swper *m.* and *f.*
support, to	cynnal *v.n.*
sure	si[r, sicr
surmise, to	tybio
surprise	syndod *m.*
swallow, to	llyncu *v.n.*
swan	alarch (elyrch)
sweat	chwys
sweat, to	chwysu *v.n.*
swede	rwden (rwdins)
sweep, to	ysgubo *v.n.*
sweet	melys (-ion)
swift	cyflym
swim, to	nofio *v.n.*
swimming pool	pwll nofio
swimsuit	dillad nofio
swing, to	siglo *v.n.*
sword	cleddyf (-au) *m.*
symbol	arwydd (-ion) *m.*

T

table	bwrdd (byrddau) *m.*
tablecloth	lliain bwrdd
tablet	tabled (-i)
tail	cynffon (-nau) *f.*
take, to	cymeryd *v.n.*
tale	chwedl (-au)
tall	tal
tame	dôf
tame, to	dofi *v.n.*
tank	tanc
tapestry	brethyn cartref
tart	tarten
taste, to	blasu *v.n.*
tasty	blasus
tavern	tafarn (-au) *f.*
tea	tê *m.*
teach, to	dysgu *v.n.*
teacher	athro *m.*, athrawes *f.* (athrawon)
teapot	tebot (-iau) *m.*
tear	deigryn (dagrau) *m.*
tear, to	rhwygo *v.n.*
teaspoon	llwy de *m.*
telephone	teleffôn

string	llinyn (-nau) *m.*
tell, to	dweud *v.n.*
temper	tymer *f.*
tempestuous	tymhestlog
ten	deg
tent	pabell (pebyll) *f.*
tenant	deiliad (deiliaid)
thank, to	diolch *v.n.*
the	y, yr
their	eu
them	nhw, hwy
then	yna
there	yno
these	rhain
they	nhw
thick	tew, trwchus
thickness	trwch
thief	lleidr (lladron) *m.*
thin	tenau
thing	peth (-au) *m.*
think, to	meddwl *v.n.*
thirst	syched
thirteen	un deg tri
this	hwn *m.*, hon *f.*
thousand	mil (-oedd) *f.*
threat	bygythiad (-au)
threaten, to	bygwth *v.n.*
three	tri
throne	gorsedd *f.*
through	drwy
throw, to	taflu *v.n.*
thumb	bawd (bodiau) *m.*
thunder	taran (-nau) *f.*
Thursday	dydd Iau
ticket	tocyn (-nau) *m.*
tide	llanw
tie	tei *m.* and *f.*
tie, to	clymu, rhwymo *v.n.*
time	amser (-au) *m.*
tin	tun (-iau) *m.*
tire, to	blino *v.n.*
tired	blinedig
to	i, at
toast	tôst
tobacco	baco
today	heddiw
toilet	toiled, t] bach
tomato	tomato (-s) *f.*
tomorrow	yfory
tongue	tafod (-au) *m.*
tonight	heno
ton	tunnell (tunelli)
too	rhy, hefyd
tool	offeryn (offer) *m.*
tooth	dant (dannedd) *m.*
toothache	dannodd *f.*
toothbrush	brws dannedd
toothpaste	past dannedd
touch, to	cyffwrdd *v.n.*
touring	teithiol

television	teledu *m.*
towards	tuag at
towel	llian (llineiniau) *f.*
tower	t[r (tyrau) *m.*
town	tref (-i) *f.*
toy	tegan (-nau) *m.*
trade	masnach *f.*
tradition	traddodiad (-au) *m.*
traffic	traffig
train	trén (-au) *m.*
tramp	cardotyn *m.*
translate, to	cyfieithu *v.n.*
travel, to	teithio *v.n.*
traveller	teithiwr (teithwyr) *m.*
tree	coeden (coed) *f.*
trouble	helynt (-ion) *f.*
trousers	trowsus
trout	brithyll
true	gwir
trust	ymddiriedaeth
trust, to	ymddiried *v.n.*
truth	gwirionedd
try, to	ymdrechu, ceisio *v.n.*
Tuesday	dydd Mawrth
tune	tôn (-nau) *f.*
turkey	twrci
turn	tro (-eon) *m.*
turn, to	troi *v.n.*
turnip	meipen
twelve	un deg dau
twenty	dau ddeg
twig	brigyn (brigau) *m.*
two	dau *m.*, dwy *f.*
tyre	teiar (-s) *m.*

U

ugly	hyll
umbrella	ambarel
unbearable	annioddefol
uncle	ewythr *m.*
under	dan
understand, to	deall *v.n.*
union	undeb (-au) *m.*
unite, to	uno *v.n.*
unlucky	anlwcus
until	tan, hyd nes
up	i fyny, lan
upright	syth
use, to	defnyddio *v.n.*
useful	defnyddiol

V

vaccination	frech *f.*
valley	cwm (cymoedd) *m.*
	dyffryn (-oedd) *m.*
van	fan (-iau)
vanity	oferedd *m.*
variety	amrywiaeth (-au) *m.*
various	amryw
veal	cig llo

tow, to	tynnu *v.n.*
verse	pennill (penillion) *m.*
verse (Bible)	adnod (-au) *f.*
very	iawn
vicar	ficer (-i) *m.*
victorious	buddugol
victory	buddugoliaeth
village	pentref (-i)
visit, to	ymweld â *v.n.*
vocal	llafur
voice	llais (lleisiau) *m.*

W

wages	cyflog (-au) *m.* and *f.*
wait, to	aros *v.n.*
wake, to	deffro *v.n.*
Wales	Cymru
walk, to	cerdded *v.n.*
wall	wal (-iau) *f.*
	mur (-iau) *f.*
wander, to	crwydro *v.n.*
want, to	eisiau *v.n.*
war	rhyfel (-oedd) *m.*
warden	warden
warm	cynnes
warn, to	rhybuddio *v.n.*
warning	rhybudd (-ion) *m.*
wash, to	ymolchi *v.n.*
watch	oriawr
watch, to	gwylio *v.n.*
water	dŵr (dyfroedd) *m.*
water, to	dyfrio *v.n.*
watercress	berw d[r
wave (sea)	ton (-nau) *f.*
wave, to	chwifio *v.n.*
way	ffordd
we	ni, ninnau
weak	gwan
wear, to	gwisgo *v.n.*
weather	tywydd *m.*
wedding	priodas
Wednesday	dydd Mercher
week	wythnos (-au) *f.*
weep, to	wylo, crio *v.n.*
weigh, to	pwyso *v.n.*
weight	pwysau
welcome	croeso *m.*
welcome, to	croesawu *v.n.*
well	ffynnon (ffynhonnau) *f.*
Welsh (language)	Cymraeg *f.*
Welsh (people)	Cymro (Cymry) *m.*
west	gorllewin
wet	gwlyb
wet, to	gwlychu *v.n.*
what	beth
whatever	beth bynnag
wheat	gwenith
wheel	olwyn (-ion)
when	pryd
where	ble

vegetables	llysiau
whirlwind	corwynt (-oedd)
whisky	chwisgi *m.*
whistle	chwiban
whistle, to	chwibannu *v.n.*
white	gwyn
whiting	gwyniad
who	pwy
whole	cyfan, holl, cwbl
why	pam
wide	llydan, eang
width	llêd
wife	gwraig (gwragedd) *f.*
wild	gwyllt
willow	helygen
win, to	ennill *v.n.*
wind	gwynt (-oedd) *m.*
window	ffenestr (-i) *f.*
windy	gwyntog
wine	gwin (-oedd) *m.*
winter	gaeaf (-au) *m.*
with	gyda
witness	tyst (-ion) *m.*
witness, to	tystio *v.n.*
woman	dynes, merch (merched
wonder, to	synnu *v.n.*
wonderful	rhyfeddol
wood	coed, coedwig *m.*
wood (piece)	pren (-iau) *m.*
woodwork	gwaith coed
wool	gwlân

while	tra
word	gair (geiriau) *m.*
work	gwaith (gweithiau) *m.*
work, to	gweithio *v.n.*
workmen	gweithwyr *m.*
world	byd (-oedd) *m.*
worship, to	addoli *v.n.*
worth	gwerth
wound	clwyf (-au) *m.*
wound, to	clwyfo *v.n.*
wretch	truan (trueiniaid) *m.*
wriggle, to	ymwingo *v.n.*
wrist	garddwrn
write, to	ysgrifennu *v.n.*
wrong	anghywir

Y

yacht	cwch hwylio
yard (measure)	llathen (-ni), llath
yard	iard, cwrt
year	blwyddyn (blynydd-oedd) *f.*
year, last	llynedd
year, this	eleni
yell, to	gweiddi *v.n.*
yellow	melyn
yesterday	ddoe
yew tree	ywen
you	chwi
young	ifanc, ieuanc
your	eich

From its origins in the European Celtic heartlands a thousand years earlier, the Welsh language emerged as a written and spoken language in Wales in the 5th and 6th centuries. The age of the Christian missionaries followed, with patron saint David spreading the preaching of his austere faith from his monastery in south-west Wales. The Welsh became a People, protecting themselves from attacks from the east.

The Danish attacked from the sea; Rhodri fawr (Rhodri the Great) in 851 organised defences. In 1067 the Normans entered South Wales and built the first castles and towns. In 1100 Henry becomes king and the Normans expanded in Pembrokeshire and Glamorgan. In 1140, Owain Gwynedd drove foreigners out of North Wales, and in the south, Rhys ap Gryffydd dominated from his seat at Dynefor Castle. In 1165 Henry II formed a huge army, attacked Wales, and Wales united; Henry's army was defeated in the Berwyn Mountains. Rhys held a gathering of bards in 1177 at Cardigan, the first Eisteddfod. Llewellyn ap Iorweth (Llewellyn the Great) became leader of North Wales, negotiating with King John, winning rights in the Magna Carta; he died in 1240. His grandson Llewellyn 'Prince of Wales' was recognised by Henry III in the Treaty of Montgomery, becoming the first and only Welsh Prince of Wales In 1277 Edward I's army marched into Wales; a harsh peace treaty was signed at Rhuddlan. Edward's huge castles could be provisioned from the sea, and secured English influence. Llewellyn tried to raise support in the South from his base at Aberedw Castle; on his way north to re-join his supporters the Prince of Wales ran in to a group of English soldiers and was killed. His statue stands near Builth Wells. His brother Dafydd was hung, drawn and quartered at Shrewsbury.

Edward built four huge castles (1283-1300): Harlech; Conwy; Caernarfon and Beaumaris. The revolt of Owain Glyndwr, immortalized by Shakespeare, started with his attack on Ruthin in September 21st, 1400. Henry IV was unable to quell the rebellion, and the whole of Wales rose under one ruler. The French joined the Welsh and combined troops marched eastwards as far as Worcester. But in 1410 Owain Glyndwr was forced into hiding and was not seen again.

In 1485 Henry Tudor landed at Milford Haven with an army of largely Frenchmen; he marched through Wales and within 20 days he defeated Richard III at Bosworth, near Leicester, and took the English throne. He was the first of the three great Tudor monarchs, with their origins in Anglesey, who ruled Britain until the death of Elizabeth I in 1603.

WELSH LANGUAGE (Cymraeg): A member of the Celtic branch of the Indo-European language family. Its origins lie in europe in pre-Roman times, which makes it the oldest surviving language in Europe. It belongs to the Brythonic group of Celtic languages, along with Breton and Cornish. The surviving Celtic languages of Scotland (Gaelic) and of Ireland are of the Goidelic group. Welsh is spoken by c.720,000 people in Wales, about one-quarter of the population.

WELSH LITERATURE: this was well developed before the Norman Conquest. Four late 6th century bards' works are preserved in ancient manuscripts. the tradition of writing in Wales is largely of poetry writing. In the 14th century the South Wales poet Dafydd ap Gwilym broke the classical eulogistic traditions and wrote more freely. Early modern Welsh prose standards were partly set by Bishop Morgan's 1583 translation of the Bible. Religious feeling and the interest of the clergy kept the language alive in the 18th Century. The great Methodist hymnodists William Williams (Pantycelyn) and Ann Griffiths created hymns which are sung in Welsh chapels and at rugby games today. In the 19th Century the local novels of Mold-based Daniel Owen were widely read, and in the 20th Century the novels and short stories of Kate Roberts, based on the slate-quarrying areas south of Caernarfon, are regarded as classics, especially the short novel 'Traed Mewn Cyffion', now available in English translation as 'Feet in Chains'.

POLITICS: The long tradition of Wales is one of regional differences, tribal warfare and no unifying leadership (apart from two all-Wales movements, one under Owain Glyndwr, a Border aristocrat, starting in Ruthin in 1401 and lasting about ten years, in which the first Welsh parliament was created at Machynlleth). In 1999, under the National Assembly of Wales, a devolved government for Wales has started to function from its HQ in Cardiff. It has significant power and is entirely responsible for funding and administering Health, Education and other areas in Wales. There are 40 members of the Welsh Assembly (AMs), each (as in the case of MP's) representing constituencies, elected by ballot and 20 Members allocated by a PR system.

The Welsh Assembly (2014) is now calling itself a Parliament. It has been allowed by the UK Parliament in London to create its own laws. In Wales, prescription charges have been abolished. In an important move towards re-cycling, shoppers in Wales have to pay a fee (passed on to charities) if they receive their goods in a bag.

The Welsh Assembly has (in 2014) a budget of c£12.5 billion, with c£9 billion spent on Health: the other portion mostly spent on Education and Local Administration.

THE LANGUAGE: Recent details show a decline in Welsh-speakers in Wales. In the Nineteenth Century, over half the Welsh population spoke Welsh. Since then there has been a steady decline, although the population has increased to the present c3m. The 2001 census recorded 582,000 speakers; the 2011 showed a decline to £562,000, about 19% of the population. The Welsh-speaking heartlands, Ceredigion and Carmarthenshire, showed a significant drop. It is estimated that 133,000 Welsh speakers live in England, about 50,000 in Greater London and 2,500 in the USA. The total number of Welsh-speakers appears to be in the region of 720,000.

Cardiff is the Capital City of Wales. A small increase in Welsh-speaking was recorded here in the 2011 census. It includes the HQ broadcasting companies, with BBC Wales equipped with extensive film-making studios at Cardiff Bay. Here the Assembly Senedd building is architecturally outstanding, designed by Richard Rogers Partnership. It has a section which is open for visitors.

SPORT: At the time of writing, both Cardiff and Swansea have teams in the Football Premier Division, Newport are in the Third Division with Wrexham in the league directly below. Glamorgan are the only Welsh team in the English Cricket League, with many local teams in North Wales playing in the five division North Wales Cricket League.

CULTURE: The Welsh National Opera Company works at a high level, making a significant contribution to UK music. Bryn Terfel (from near Caernarfon) is a world-renowned bass-baritone and Llyr Williams (from Wrexham) is a pianist of renown. In Literature Dylan Thomas (1914-53) is outstanding: his home at Laugharne, near Carmarthen in S.W. Wales, can be visited.